# Christ in Multidimensional Context

**Christian Heritage Rediscovered**

The Series, as the name suggests, is meant to focus on Christian Faith & Living vis-à-vis topics like Literature & Poetry, Indigenous Philosophizing, Ethical response towards Agriculture, Health & Healing, Science & Technology, Ecofeminist Theology, Sociological approach towards Human Rights, Law & Politics, Arts, History of Ideas, Ancient Civilizations, Cultural Contiguity, Religious Cosmologies & Mysticism, Footsteps of famous Theologians, world Peace & Harmony, Global Capitalism, Network Marketing, Cybertheology, Population & Demographics, Epigraphic Studies, Contextualized Education, and many others. We welcome a Mss. on any topic/s mentioned, whether they are original works, scholarly monographs, collections of conference papers, revised dissertations, or translations of historical documents. Through the Series we, the Publishers, are striving to put forward published works that may help Institutions, Academic Bodies, Researchers, Scholars and the world at large in furthering their respective knowledge and understanding on the concerned subject. We welcome your comments on our efforts and further suggestions on how we can foster the upcoming thoughtful theologically grounded books.

*Christian Heritage Rediscovered - 15*

# Christ in Multidimensional Context

## *An Integrated Presentation of Articles*

**Rev. Amit Thomas**
*Department of Christian Theology*
*Allahabad Bible Seminary, Allahabad*

CWI
**Christian World Imprints**(TM)

First Published in 2015 by

**Christian World Imprints**(TM)
*Christian Publishing & Books from India*
H-12 Bali Nagar, **New Delhi-110015**
info@christianworldimprints.com
www.ChristianWorldImprints.com
Phone: +91 11 25465925 Fax: +91 11 25173055

ISBN-13: 978-93-5148-037-2 ISBN-10: 93-5148-037-2

**Cataloging in Publication Data--DK**
Courtesy: D.K. Agencies (P) Ltd. <docinfo@dkagencies.com>

**Thomas, Amit,** 1975- **author**.
Christ in multidimensional context : an integrated presentation of articles / Rev. Amit Thomas (Allahabad Bible Seminary).
pages cm. -- (Christian heritage rediscovered ; 15)
Includes bibliographical references (pages ) and index.
ISBN 9789351480372
ISBN 9351480372

1. Jesus Christ. 2. Theology. I. Title. II. Series: Christian heritage rediscovered ; 15.

DDC 232 23



Printed at Chawla Offset Printers

Dedicated to my beloved wife Ashita and
sons Anant & Arman, my faithful companions
who supported me through their love,
cooperation and labour.

# The Book

The book makes an attempt to understand Christ from different perspectives in the contemporary world. It tries to survey, both traditional as well as contemporary understanding of the subject and their relevance in the present day situation. This book is an outcome of much discussions and enormous reading. It explores the problem of religious language in theology and historical understanding of Christ as well as His contemporary view & its relevance. It calls for the theology to begin from the context and bottom not necessarily always from the transcendental level.

The Author has also showcased the teaching efforts and articles written and presented at different times by the esteemed personalities of this genre. He challenges us to be more active in understanding Christ from different parameters vis a vis the changed scenario of the modern world. The Author believes that Christ needs to be brought forth as a force of liberation and be embodied in all the changed situations, where still the unjust social structures suffocate people to live and grow.

This book is meant to be a handy tool for both the socio-theological fraternity as well as lay leadership, alike.

# The Author

Rev. Amit Thomas, having completed his M.A from Kashi Vidhyapeeth (University), Varanasi, and B.D. and M.Th. degree from U.B.S and NIIPGTS (University of Serampore), is teaching in the Department of Christian Theology, Allahabad Bible Seminary, Allahabad, since 2001. He has also presented several articles in different journals.

# Foreword

Explorations on thematic issues in sixteen short essays wide ranging from Religious language, Hermeneutic, God, Sin, Atonement, Christology salvation, Kingdom of God, Black and Tribal theology through the eyes of Augustine, Thomas Aquinas, Paul Tillich, Karl Barth, Rudolph Bultmann, James Cone, Sebastian Kappen, and M. M. Thomas is commendable. The author is a theological educator as well as a research scholar. In between teaching and research, his effort of writing the work and getting it published is quite commendable and encouraging.

In one of the essays pertinently he draws attention to "the thought of a new community which is valid to present a new fellowship of mutual forgiveness created by Divine forgiveness in Christ expressed in the Eucharist and social 'koinonia' of the church as the foretaste of true human community as the essential gospel". It highlights the call for an engagement of the Church in the world. The essays try to address each issue from a particular perspective without interlinking them with any common thread. Not the least he cites and gives a challenging call with the statement of Jesus "whosoever would be great among you must be your servant, and whoever would be first among you must be the slave of all " should not be interpreted as mere advice but a call to radically renounce all exercise of power.

It is my pleasure to write the 'FOREWORD' with the hope that the initiative of taking a small step in search for truth as well as offering all essays in one volume for public reading will benefit the readers and in particular students of this genre.

**Bishop D.K.Sahu**
Dean-Director
Faculty of Theology
SHIATS Deemed University
Allahabad, India

# Acknowledgements

At the very outset, I want to thank the almighty God for his ever present help without which it would have not been possible to do this work. God's grace has enabled me to take up this subject. Along the side, there had been many people who had been a source of inspiration for me during my life journey. I would like to express my heartfelt thanks to my wife Ashita and children Anant & Arman, without their support I would have not been able to take this work. I also want to equally thank my parents Rev. Arvind Thomas and Beulah Thomas for their endless love and support that was rendered to me always. I also thank Marilyn Collins for her love and encouragement that she gave to me time to time for this work.

For this multidisciplinary study and research my grateful thanks are due to Rev. Dr. Sunil M. Caleb, Principal, Bishop's College; Rev. Dr. Ivy Singh and Dr. Somen Das who have been a source of inspiration and guidance. I also would attest a word of thanks for the encouragement and valuable suggestions received from Rev. J Sundara Raj, Principal Allahabad Bible Seminary and Dr. John V. Mathew, Assist. Professor, Department of Religion and Philosophy, Allahabad Bible Seminary.

I am immensely grateful to Christian World Imprints and its editorial staff for, for their support and help, and undiminished commitment for getting the book published. God bless you all!

**Rev. Amit Thomas**
Allahabad
Uttar Pradesh

# Introduction

Many of us who have been writing the theology are not conscious of what are the things that happen around us many times. Many of us do theology but are unaware about the discussions outside of our classrooms. We are comfortable within our four closet boundaries of thinking and thus sometimes we fail to understand the Multidimensional contexts in which we live. I have been teaching in the area of Christian theology, so it's a delight for me that I got the opportunity to publish this work. This book is the fruit of my teaching and research which I have been doing in the past years. My discussion with people around the globe, Church leaders and Theologians suggests that everywhere we are wrestling with the question: How to understand Christ in Multidimensional contexts?

The context undergoes many changes and as a result, different new awareness about the reality comes into light. As the title suggests, this book aims to get into the different discussions and see Christ from the Multidimensional perspectives. This book is basically the teaching efforts and collections of articles written and presented at different times. They deal primarily with the Christ as a Person & His Works, and how Christ understanding is relevant from different spheres of life. It also presents the challenges which are brought forth to us for doing theology in the given context.

I have desired that these writings will help the socio-theological fraternity to pounder and think upon Christ's Multidimensional aspect and brings His relevance for the humanity as whole. The fact of the matter is that there are many discussions about Christ and sometimes we are even misled but these writings would help us to be more than a reader. This book will be helpful in taking up the challenge of understanding Christ in different directions. In order to have Multidimensional understanding of Christ, I have taken into consideration firstly, the historical understanding of Christ and then the western view, and later the Asian and Indian view as a whole. I aspire always that our theology should be from the bottom not from the transcended level which sometime becomes obscure and less challenging.

***"For with you is the fountain of life;***
***In your light we see light"***
***(Psalm 36:9)***

# Contents

Chapter I

# Methodological Issues: Religious Language in Theology

## Introduction

Perhaps at no time a Christian theologian would feel more challenged to do theology in a novel way than in the context of the sufferings and struggles of both human and nature. Utterances made in religious contexts are of many sorts. It is true that there is s religious language and those religious terms and phrases had been a problem from early time. In the performance of public and private worship men engage in acts of praise, petition, thanks, confession and exhortation. In Sacred writings we find historical records, dramatic narratives, proclamation of law, predictions, admonitions, evaluations and theological pronouncements. In devotional literature there are rules of conduct, biographical narratives and thoughts of religious experience. "Philosophical talks of religious language have focused on a restricted segment of this great diversity, such as theological assertions of the existence, nature and doing of supernatural personal being."[1] The works of the recent past scholars have given some light on this issue which has enabled us to think and come to some conclusions. In order to understand the complexity of the problem of religious language we will look to some thinkers and their views and will try to see the nature of religious language, the Doctrine of analogy (Aquinas), religious statements as symbolic (Paul Tillich), religious language as form of life, incarnation and the problem of meaning, religious language as noncognitive and analysis of religious language.

## Nature of Religious Language

Religious language is characterized by complexity. Sometimes it is more complex than the language of science. The crucial problems about religious languages appear in their purest form in theological statements. It is the concept of communication with supernatural person that seems unclear. We may say that the difficulties in understanding other forms of religious language stem from unclear statements about God. "The philosophical concentration on the theological statements lies in the fact that Philosophy of religion is primarily concerned with the question of justifiability, significance and value."[2] Thus, the Philosophy of religion is largely taken up with the examining the grounds of religious statements. When we see this we realize the puzzling aspects of religious language.

The complexity of the religious language is evident from the admission of the sentences of three categories: "First, sentences asserting the nature and existence of God- they are truth asserting statements. Second, sentences which express complex of feeling towards that one prays to and third, sentences which indicate the commitment to a certain way of life."[3] In this view, God is the centre to religious language. The two main issues are raised by recent scholars: one which was familiar to the medieval thinkers and which is being actively investigated with new philosophical techniques

1 William P. Alston, "Religious language", *The Encyclopedia of Philosophy*, edited by Paul Edwards, vol. 7 (1967): 168.

2 Ibid., 169.

3 Santosh Chandra Sengupta, *Logic of Religious Language* (Calcutta: Prajna, 1978), 21.

today, concerns the special sense that descriptive terms bar when they are used for God. The other pressing question, which also has a long history, is concerned with the basic function of the religious language. "The terms which are applied in the religious predicates to God are being used in special ways, differing from their use in ordinary day to day contexts."[4]

## Meaning of Theological Predicates

The predicates are essential to the religious language. The predicates are meaningful in their particular context which a express complex of feelings. This feeling can be awe, attachment, and love. Most of the philosophers find the difficulties of religious language in connection with the theological affirmations. (What does "good" mean in "God is good") Theological predicates can be seen in two: Negative- infinite, nontemporal, incorporeal, and positive- the predicates concerned either with attributes (good, wise, omniscient) or with actions (makes, forgives, speaks and watchers over). When we reflect on the use of predicates in the theological statements we realize that these predicates are mainly derived from the application of the predicates to human beings and other observable titles. The difference in the use of predicates as applied to God and human beings, there are many ways of seeing that the terms cannot have quiet the same in both cases. In the classical Christian theology, God is conceived of as not in time, than it is clear that God's performance of action like speaking, making or comforting is something radically different from the temporally sequential performance of action by human beings. Since, God is in corporeal, his speaking cannot involve producing sounds by expelling air over vocal cords.

We also find in the religious language the paradox predicates. For example: 'God is manifest and unmanifest'; 'God is far and near'; 'God is beyond God'; God is personal and 'impersonal'. "The attribution of the seemingly opposite predicates to the same object in each case is not a case of contradiction as they refer to the different aspects of the comprehensive being that God is to be in different

4 John H. Hick, *Philosophy of Religion* (New Jersey: Prentice-Hall, INC, 1963), 78.

relationships in which God can be viewed."[5] For instance, 'manifest' in the sentence 'God is manifest and unmanifest', manifest refers to the aspect of God that is revealed in the world while unmainfest indicates the aspect of Divine being, which is hidden. So, we can speak of God although not in the manner we speak of an ordinary object.

## The Doctrine of Analogy (Aquinas)

Great scholars and thinkers were well aware of religious language problem so they developed the idea of analogy to deal with the problem. "The doctrine of "analogical predication", as it occurs in Aquinas and his commentator Cajetan is not difficult to grasp."[6] He says that when a word, such as 'good' is applied to both: a created being and God, it is not being used univocally (i.e., with exactly the same meaning) in the two cases. God is not good, for example, in identically the sense in which human being may be good. No, on the other hand, do we apply the adjective "good", to God and man equivocally (i.e., with completely different and unrelated meanings), as when the bat is used to refer both to the flying animal and to the instrument used in baseball. There is definite connection between God's goodness and man, reflecting the fact that God has created man. According to Aquinas then, "good", is applied to Creator and Creature, neither univocally nor equivocally but analogically. The understanding of this can be seen if we consider first an analogy "downwards from man to the lower form of life".

We sometimes say of a pet dog that is faithful, and we may also describe a man as faithful. We use the same word in each case because of similarity between a certain quality exhibited in the behavior of the dog and the steadfast voluntary adherence to a person or a cause which we call faithfulness in human beings. Because of this similarity we are not using the word faithful equivocally (with totally difference sense). But on the other hand, there is an immense difference in quality between a dog's attitude and man's. The one is surely superior to the other in respect of responsibility, self conscious deliberation

5 Sengupta, op. cit, 33.

6 Hick, op. cit, 79.

and relating of attitudes to moral purposes and ends. Because of this difference we are not using "faithful", univocally (in exactly the same sense). We are using it analogically, to show that at the level of dog's consciousness there is a quality which is corresponds to what at human level we call faithfulness. "There is a recognizable likeness in structure of attitudes or patterns that causes us to use the same word for both man and animal."[7] There is thus both similarity within difference and difference within similarity of the kind that led Aquinas to speak of the analogical use of the same term in two very different contexts.

In the case of our analogy "Downwards", true or normative faithfulness is that which we know directly in ourselves and dim and imperfect faithfulness of dog is known only by analogy. But in the case of the analogy "Upwards" from man to God, the situation is reversed. It is our own directly goodness, love, wisdom, etc., which are the thin shadows and remote approximation, and the perfect qualities of Godhead that are known to us only by analogy. Thus, when we say that God is good, we are telling that there is a quality of infinite perfect being that corresponds to what at our human level we call goodness. In this case, this is the Divine goodness which is the true, normative and unbroken reality, while human life shows at best a faint, fragmentary, and distorted reflection of this quality. Only in God can the perfections of the being occur in their true and unfractured nature: only God knows, love, and is righteous and wise in the full and proper sense.

The Doctrine of analogy doesn't profess to bring out the concrete character of God's perfections, but only to indicate the relation between the different meanings of word when it is applied both to men and (on the basis of revelation) God. Analogy is not an instrument for exploring and mapping the infinite Divine nature; it is an account of the way in which terms are used of the deity. "The Doctrine of analogy provides a framework for certain limited statements about God, without infringing upon agnosticism. And the sense of the mystery of the Divine being, which have always characterized Christian and Jewish thought at their best."[8]

7 Hick, op. cit, 80.

8 Ibid., 81.

## Religious Statements as Symbolic (Paul Tillich)

An important element in the thought of Paul Tillich is his doctrine of the "symbolic" nature of religious language. "Tillich distinguishes between a sign and a symbol and both of it point to something else beyond themselves."[9] But a sign signifies that to which it points by arbitrary convention- for example, when the red light at the street corner shows that the drivers are asked to stop. In contrast to this purely external connection, a symbol "participates in that to which it points."[10] To use Tillich example, a flag participates in the power and dignity of the nation which it represents. Because of this inner connection with the reality symbolized, symbols are not arbitrary instituted, like conventions sign, but grow out of the individual or collective conscious. "A symbol opens up levels of reality which otherwise are closed to us and at the same time unlocks dimensions and elements of our soul".[11]

Tillich says that religious faith, which is the state of being "ultimate concern" about the ultimate, can only express itself in symbolic languages. Whatever we say about that which concerns us ultimately, whether or not we call it God, has a symbolic meaning. It points beyond itself while participating in that which it points. In no other way can faith express itself adequately. "The language of faith is the language of symbols".[12] There is, according to Tillich, one and only one literal, non-symbolic statement which can be made about the ultimate reality which religion calls God- that God is Being-itself. Beyond this all the theological predicates- such as, God is eternal, living, good, personal, Creator and he loves the creatures- are symbolic. "There can be no doubt that any concrete assertion about God must be symbolic, for a concrete assertion is one which uses a segment of finite experience to say something about him."[13] Tillich insists that we don't use human language literary, or

9 Hick, op. cit., 81.

10 Paul Tillich, *Dynamics of Faith* (New York: Harper & Row, publishers, Inc.), 42.

11 Ibid., 42.

12 Ibid., 45.

13 Paul Tillich, *Systematic Theology, I*, (Chicago: University of Chicago Press, 1951), 239.

univocally, when we talk about ultimate. Because our terms can only be derived from our own finite human experiences, they can't be adequate to apply for God; when used theologically, their meaning is always partially negated by that to which they point. "Religiously this doctrine constitutes a warning against the idolatry of thinking of God as though he were merely a greatly magnified human being."[14]

The application to theological predicates of Tillich's raise question of to which it is philosophical in nature. Tillich's teaching, although valuable suggestive, scarcely constitutes at this point a fully articulated philosophical position. Along with this we also find that "some symbols are expressed as metaphors which have a place in religious language."[15] In some cases, metaphor is used in a way so as to conceal its analogical character. According to "Wittgenstein a religious believer needs to learn how metaphors as pictures can be used."[16] For example, when we say that 'God, has eye over the affairs of man' the use of metaphor is legitimate. But, the utterance of eyebrow in the sentence 'God has eyebrows' does not make any sense.

## Incarnation and the Problem of Meaning

It is claimed by some that the Doctrine of the Incarnation offers the possibility of a partial solution to the problem of theological meaning. There are differences between the metaphysical attributes of God (eternity, infinity, etc.) and his moral attributes (goodness, love, wisdom, etc.). "The doctrine of incarnation involves the claim that the moral (but not metaphysical) attributes of God have been embodied, in a finite human life, namely, that of the Christ."[17] This claim makes it possible to point to the person of Christ showing what it meant by assertions such as, "God is good", and "God loves His human creatures". The moral attributes of God towards mankind are held to have been incarnated in Jesus and expressed concretely in His dealing with men and women. The incarnation doctrine involves

14 Hick, op. cit., 83.

15 Sengupta, op. cit., 27.

16 Ibid.

17 Hick, op. cit., 84.

the claim that, for example, Jesus' compassion for the sick and the spiritually blind was God's compassion for them; His forgiving of sins, God's forgiveness; and His condemnation of self righteously religious, God's condemnation of them. On the basis of this belief, the life of Christ as depicted in the New Testament records, provides a foundation for statements about God. Thus, God's love is continues in character with that displayed in the life of Jesus.

## Religious Language as Form of Life

According to Wittgenstein, language is plural. The reason for the multiplicity of language is that each language is put to a separate use and represents a separate mode of usage. "Language is like a game, it is a rule regulated activity and each language like a game is a self contained practice."[18] As games don't have common characteristics, languages do not even have common features. The religious language is separate unit of discourse. Even Wittgenstein draws another analogy to speak of religious language as a form of life. He says to imagine a language is to imagine a form of life. "The form of life does not refer to some activities in which living is involved, but to what may be called totality of the behavior."[19] The behavior referred to is not of an individual but of the people and, for that matter, way of life is a social phenomenon. So, religious language is a self contained and self sufficient discourse and as such it is a separate complex having its own criteria or logic. But, Wittgenstein thought about religious language as form of life and has criticism also such as: it is not necessary that one has to be an insider to understand the concepts of religious language. Religious language develops through interaction with other languages and so self contained and self sufficient.

## Religious Language from Indian Epistemology

Western Philosophy generally recognizes two ultimate sources of knowledge namely perception or immediate knowledge and inference or mediate knowledge. From the Indian epistemology standpoint there are six valid sources of knowledge (pramanas)

---

18 Sengupta, op. cit., 34.

19 Ibid., 35.

namely perception (pratyaksa), inference (anumana), testimony (sabda), comparison (upamana), postulation (arthapatti) and non-congnition (anupalabdhi). The religious language can be seen in terms of Sabda (Verbal Testimony), and even Upamana (comparison). "Sabda in wider sense means sound. In the narrow sense, it is sound used as a symbol for expression of some meaning, hence stands for a "word"."[20] Thus, sabda means word or words as the source of knowledge. It would then correspond to authority or testimony. So, Sabda Pramana means words as the source of knowledge. Almost all the Indian thinkers, except the Carvakas, the Bauddhas and the Vaisesikas, accept the sabda or authority as an independent and ultimate source pf knowledge. By establishing sabda as an ultimate source of knowledge, the Advaitins and many others philosophers uphold the authority of the Vedas.

In Ancient India, the indefinite sound was called dhvani and the definite and articulated sounds of human vocal organs called Varna. But, there had been problem with the meanings of the words. Does a word primarily mean a Particular (vyakti) or a Universal (jati). Different philosophical thought have their different interpretation of the word. "When we look in the meaning of sentences or predicates it shows of sabda bodha (the two isolated words – that is two Universal words when combined results in synthetic meaning)".[21] According to Indian logician, this new meaning marks the beginning of vakya or sentence. A sentence or vakya according to Indian logic must contain a subject and a predicate. The subject must have three things: being referred, being already known and being a substantive. So subject becomes substantive and predicates becomes adjective which expresses a relation. By establishing sabda as an ultimate source of knowledge , Indian Christian thinkers uphold the authority of the Bible and extra Biblical scriptures. The Indian Christian theology wholeheartedly receives not the 'Particular Jesus' but the 'Universal Jesus'. The Universal Jesus is identical with Ultimate Reality, Brahman. "Thus we have to elevate the Bible from the historical to the eternal. We have to elevate Bible from human level to super human level; from

---

20 K. P. Aleaz, *The role of Pramanas in Hindu-Christian Epistemology* (Calcutta: Punthi Pustak, 1991), 29.

21 Ibid., 33.

dogmatism to universality."[22] At Universal level there will not be any conflict between the Truth claims of the different scriptures.

Upamana (comparison), seeing a wild cow (gavaya) in the forest one forms first the judgment, this gavaya is like my cow, and then passes to the judgment 'my cow is like this gavaya'. According to the Vedintins and Mimamsakas here the first judgment is knowledge gained through perception and second knowledge is derived through the instrumentality of the perception knowledge contained in the first. "The Sankhya School holds that upamana can be shown to be a case of perception. According to it similarity between two things means the existence of some features that are common to both."[23] These identical features are perceived whether we see a gavaya or a cow. Thus, the idea of super sensible God can be imparted in terms of its similarity to the sensible. Comparison in the wider sense has ample theological use in ordinary practical life. So, it is not only the knowledge of similarity, but the knowledge of dissimilarity also is obtained through comparison.

## Religious Language as Noncognitive

When we say what we take to be fact (or deny what alleged to be fact) we are using language cognitively. "This is a hot summer", "two plus two equal four", "he is not here" are cognitive utterances. We can define cognitive sentences as one, i.e., either true or false. But there are other types of utterances which are neither true nor false because they fulfill quite a different function from that of to describe facts. "We don't ask of a swear-word, or a command. Or a baptismal formula, or a sonnet whether it is true. The function of Swear-word is to vent one's feelings, of a command, to direct some-one's actions; of "I baptize thee…," to perform a baptism."[24] The question arises of whether theological sentences such as "God's love mankind," are cognitive or noncognitive. This doubt can be seen in two ways: a) are such sentences intended by their users to be interpreted cognitively?

22 K. P. Aleaz, op. cit., 100.

23 Ibid., 54.

24 Hick, op. cit., 85.

b) Is their logical character such that they can, regardless of intention, either be true or false?

There is no doubt that as a matter of historical fact religious people have normally believed such statements as "God loves mankind" to be not only cognitive but also true. The ordinary believer had assumed that there are religious realities and facts which is related to their convictions. At present religious languages treated as noncognitive. "**J. H. Randell** conceives of religion as a human activity which, like its compeer science and arts, makes its own special contribution to man's culture."[25] The distinctive material with which religion works is a body of symbols and myths. He says religious symbols belong with social and artistic symbols. According to **Randell,** religious symbols have four fold functions: First, they arose the emotion and stir men to actions which might strengthen men's practical commitment. Second, they stimulate corporative action and thus bind a community together through a common response to its symbols. Third, they are able to communicate qualities of experience which can't be expressed by ordinary literal use of the language. Fourth, they both evoke and serve to foster and clarify man's experience of an aspect of world or the Divine. [26] In this connection Randell's position is a departure from the traditional assumptions of the western Religion. Randell theory of Religion and of the function of the religious language express with great clarity a way of thinking which in less clearly defined forms is widespread today. "This way of thinking is epitomized in the way in which the word religion (faith used as synonym) has largely come to replace the word "God"."[27] In contexts in which in former generations questions were raised and debated concerning God, His existence, attributes, and deeds, the corresponding question today typically concern Religion, its nature, functions, forms, pragmatic values. This displacement of "God" by "Religion" as the focus of wide realm of discourse has brought with its change in character of questions which are asked in this area. In this scenario, the question of truth of religious beliefs has fallen in to the background and the issue of their practical usefulness has come

25 Hick, op. cit., 86.

26 Ibid.

27 Ibid., 87.

forward to occupy the center attention. Hence, in this changing world, Religion has become an object of intensive investigation and God is perforce identified as an idea which occurs within this complex phenomenon of Religion.

In the same line of thought, there had been analysis by **R. B. Braithwaite** who suggests that religious assertions serve primarily an ethical function. The purpose of ethical statements is to express the speaker's adherence to a certain policy of action such as; he ought to do so and so, where he is using the assertion to declare that he resolves to do to the best of his ability. [28] Religious statements, likewise, express and recommend a commitment to a certain general policy or a way of life. For example, a Christian's assertion that God is Love (agape) is his indication of "… intention to follow an agapeistic way of life". Braithwaite asks when two Religions say (Christianity and Buddhism) recommend essentially the same policy for living, in what sense they are different Religion? For Braithwaite this is unimportant. The basic distinction lies in the different sets of stories which are associated in the two religions with adherence to their way of life. In sort Braithwaite say, "A religious assertion, for me, is the assertion of an intention to carry out a certain behavior policy, subsumable under a sufficient general principle to be a moral one, together with the implicit or explicit statements, but not the assertions of certain stories". [29]

## Conclusion

As the Indian Christian theology follows the footsteps of Indian Philosophy sabda which stands for word and correspondence to authority and testimony. The Scripture are superhuman and eternal not in dogmatic sense but because the words which they are composed are eternal. A word signifies not particular but a Universal class which is eternal. From the Indian view Bible is Universal and Jesus is looked s Universal Jesus not as particular Jesus. The Universal Jesus is identical with God, the Absolute. As we have seen from the above discussion, the way thinkers have employed through different

28 Hick, op. cit., 90.

29 Ibid., 91.

examples have made clear the reading in the problem of religious languages. In order to render distinctive style of life both attractive and rational, religious beliefs must be regarded as assertions of facts, not merely as imaginative fictions. Thus, we can conclude with the remark that the works and contributions of the thinkers are worth appreciable.

## Chapter II

# Concept of Sin within Traditional Understanding

### Introduction

Aurelius Augustine lived from A.D. 354-430. His influence not only overshadowed the next thousands years but all periods ever since. His thought was seminal for the development of Western Christianity, his moral values and personal piety remained norm for the medieval and reformed Europe. St. Augustine was the last great thinker of the patristic age in the West. His was dominant influence until the thirteenth century, when it was shared, but never overthrown, by the systems inspired by Aristotle.[30] Augustine has influenced greatly people by his theology and concepts and thus his thoughts served as basis in many areas for the medieval thinkers. We will try to see in brief about Medieval Philosophy and Augustine's influence on Thomas Aquinas's theological thinking.

30 Gordon Leff, *Medieval Thought: From St. Augustine to Ockham* (Middlesex: The Campfield Press, 1958), 46.

## I. The Medieval Philosophy

Philosophy did not begin with the Middle Ages, but the Middle Ages are a good point to begin an account of Philosophy and the Christian faith. In the Middle Ages there was scarcely any import thinker who did not take Philosophy seriously. During this time there were many questions asked such as, Does God exist? How do we know? What proof we have? And many more. It is believed that Middle Age spans the thousands years from fifth to the fifteenth centuries. They have roots in the early Church and stretch out as far as the age of Renaissance and the Reformation.[31]

In the beginning of the history many Church Fathers didn't entertained Philosophy and even denounced it as root of all heresy.[32] The most outstanding thinker of early period was Augustine (354-430), the saintly Bishop of Hippo in North Africa. It was not Philosophy but his encounter with Christ which brought meaning to his life. The Word of God had chief influence on him. It has been said that both Catholicism and Protestantism stem from Augustine. The former takes from him its high view of the Church and the Sacraments. The latter follows Augustine in his vision of the sovereignty of God, man's lostness in sin and the grace of God which alone can bring Salvation to man.[33] Another idea which dominated was the concepts of Aristotle. Another person who followed Augustine was **Boethius** (470-525), a Roman who wrote his work in the prison "*on the consolation of Philosophy* which had become a classic philosophical manual. The great minds of the Middle Ages were not interested in the physical Universe for its own sake: they were interested in the reality which they believed lay behind it.

They were not much concerned about the scientific questions but were interested in the relationship between natural and the supernatural.[34] Medieval thought was a curious mixture of Christian faith and pagan Philosophy. The Church had inherited from the past

---

31 Colin Brown, *Philosophy and the Christian Faith* (London: Inter-Varsity Press, 1969), 12.

32 Ibid., 13.

33 Ibid., 15.

34 Ibid., 17-18.

its Scriptures and writers like Augustine. From them it learnt and taught Doctrines of God, Creation and Salvation. But, along with this it also inherited from Greek Philosophy, many of the best minds who were in the process of bringing together these two and produce a synthesis. Greek thought left its mark not only upon the content but also upon the form of much medieval Christian writings. Whereas Augustine was direct, personal and biblical, but medieval writings became more logical which we find at in Anselm of Canterbury, and Thomas Aquinas.

Anselm (1033-1109) born in Italy, eventually became Abbot of Bec and Archbishop of Canterbury. He is remembered for basically two thoughts: the work on atonement, "Why God became man"; theological demonstration of existence of God.[35] St. Anselm was in the direct line of descent from Augustine. They both made faith, the starting point for knowledge; they both regarded the ides of truth as evidence for its existence; they both sought for knowledge of God through eternal ideas; they both regarded the human soul as image of the Trinity. For both, reason was an instrument in demonstrating what was already believed; of itself it could not add to certitude.[36] St. Anselm's thought is dominated by what we may call the Augustinian or platonic view of truth.

## II. Thomas Aquinas's Theological Thinking

Thomas Aquinas, called the Angelic Doctor, - *doctor angelicus*, - 1225-1274, is the prince of the schoolmen, and next to St,. Augustine, the most eminent Divine of the Latin Church. He was a man of rare genius, wisdom, and purity of life.[37] He was born in 1225 coming from originally Lombard family, at the castle of Roccasecca near the small town of Aquino which lies between Naples and Rome. His mother was a Norman blood and granddaughter of the famous crusader Tancred. At five the boy was sent to the neighboring convent

35 Tony Lane, *The Lions Concise Book of Christian Thought* (Tiruvalla: Suvartha Books, 1984), 60.

36 Leff, op. cit., 99.

37 Philip Schaff, *History of the Christian Church: Nicene and post Nicene Christianity*. Vol. V, (Grand Rapids: WM. B. Eerdmans Pub., Com., 1907), 661.

of Monte Cassino from which he passed the University of Naples. In 1243, he entered the Dominican order. In 1256, became a regular Professor of theology at Paris, and taught in Bologna, Rome, and other Italian cities.[38] He died on his way to the ecumenical council of Lyons, March 7, 1274, at only forty eight years of age.

The genuine writings of Thomas Aquinas that are more than sixty, and fall into four classes: the Philosophical works are Commentaries on Aristotle's Ethics, Metaphysics and Politics; his exegetical works include Commentaries on Job, Canticles, Isaiah, the Lamentations an the Gospels; the exposition of the Gospels-consists of excerpts from the fathers; the apologetics works designed to convince the Mohammedans and other unbelievers and to promote the union of the Greeks and Latin. The most important works of Aquinas is Dogmatic Theology which includes *Summa Theological.* Thomas also made important contribution to the liturgy and hymnology.[39] Thomas intended the Summa Theologia to take place of Lombard's *Sentences* as an elementary introduction to dogma tics. Peter Lombard's material is largely drawn from Augustine and his explicit principles of organization are derived from him as well.[40]

With Augustine and John Calvin, Thomas Aquinas shares the distinction of being one of the three master theological minds of the Western World. Thomas did great work of medieval Church by giving theology a perfect form. He was not a great scholar and like Augustine, he knew no Hebrew and little Greek. Thomas had as his chief authorities Augustine and Aristotle.[41] In Thomas thought, theology and psychology are bound together as in a Sacred Science: "Sacred Science is an impress on our own minds of God's Knowledge" (*Summa Theologica* I.3).[42] In the light this context we will try to see the influence of Augustine on Thomas Aquinas Theology.

---

38 F. C. Copleston, *Aquinas* (Middlesex: Penguins Books, 1961), 9-10.

39 Philip Schaff, op. cit., 663-664.

40 W. J. Hankey, *God in Himself: Aquinas Doctrine of God as Expounded in the Summa Theologiae* (Oxford: Oxford University Press, 1987), 23.

41 Philip Schaff, op. cit., 665.

42 W. B. Monahan, *The Psychology of St. Thomas Aquinas* (London: Ebenezer & Sons Ltd., 2000), 16.

## A. The Concept of Original Sin

According to **Augustine,** man came from the hand of his maker, his genuine masterpiece, without the slightest fault. He possessed freedom, to do good; reason, to know God. The paradise was not only spiritual, but also visible and material, without heat or cold, without weariness or excitement, without sickness, pains or defects of any kind.[43] Augustine makes important distinction between possibility of not sinning and impossibility of sinning. The former is the conditional or potential freedom from sin, which may turn into bondage of sin. This belongs to man before the fall. The latter is the absolute freedom from sin or the perfected holiness, which belongs to God and angels. The essence of sin of Adam consisted not in the eating of the fruit; but in disobedience to command of God.

So original sin according to Augustine, is the native bent of the soul towards evil, with which all the posterity of Adam-excepting Christ, come into the World, and out of which all actual sins of necessity proceed. As sin is not merely a thing of the body but essentially of the spirit we need to see which view Augustine held for the origin of soul: Traducian or Generation theory/the Creation theory/ the Pre-existence theory. In this regard Augustine rejects the Pre-existence theory but hangs between Creationism and Traducianism and brings the state of ignorance. He says this is the area of science and schools.[44] Augustine basis his thought on Rom 5: 12 that, "in Adam all have sinned".

In this view, Thomas Aquinas rejects the Traducian theory and accepts the Creationist. He says soul is the inward man. The

---

43 Philip Schaff, *History of the Christian Church: Nicene and post Nicene Christianity*. Vol. III, (Grand Rapids: WM. B. Eerdmans Pub., Com., 1910), 818.

44 Ibid., 830-832. **Traducian** teaches that the soul originates with the body from the act of procreation therefore through human agency.this is held by many Western theologians for this doctrine. The **Creation** theory ascribes each soul to direct creative act of God, and supposes it to be united with the body either at the moment of its generation, or afterwards. This view is mostly held by Eastern theologians and even Pelagius held this view. **The Pre-existence** which was held by Plato and developed by Origen. This suppose that soul even before the origin of body existed and sinned in another world, and has been banished in the body.

beginning of the man is by generation, is like that of animal, for they are made of Earth. And in this sense human soul is corruptible (*Summa Theologica* I. 75, 4&6).[45] Thomas says original sin is a disorder of the moral constitution and shows itself in concupiscence that is irrational desire. This shows the corrupt condition of the body as sickness. So, the cause of sin was an inordinate love for self. It is disability and disablement. Original sin is the loss of that balance of nature and integrity in which God created Adam. It is this certain weakness of nature which permits sin to dwell in us. He says all men born out of Adam may be called one man, by having common nature, and the will of Adam is imputed to all. The original sin is not the sin of the individual person except this person receives the nature from the parent. Thus, each soul is new Creation for its own body.[46] So, in Thomas view the corruption of nature is partial, a wound not total deadness of the moral nature. In this regard, Thomas partly basis his thought pattern on Augustine concept but differs in telling that human soul is corruptible.

## B. The Sacrament

The sacraments are visible signs of invisible things, as Augustine defined them. Any teaching of Augustine and Thomas Aquinas arouses so much revolt in the Christian theology of this age as the teaching about the future estate of unbaptized children dying in infancy. These theologians agree in denying to them all hope of the future bliss. They are detained in hell for the sin of the Adam. The Sacrament of faith, that is baptism, not being applied to them, they are forever lost. Baptism liberates from the original sin, and without baptism there is no Salvation (Summa Theologica III. 57, 7).[47] On the baptism stand Thomas fully depends upon Augustine,

45 Anton C. Pegis, ed., *Introduction to Saint Thomas Aquinas* (New York: The modern Library, 1945), 285-287.

46 W.B. Monahan, op. cit., 25-27. Thomas held that arrival of rational soul occurs when the embryo has been sufficiently developed to become the appropriate material constitutent of the human being. This rational soul has gradual development, from vegetative soul to the feeling soul as in animal soul and only after birth revealing higher rational faculty.

47 Philip Schaff, op.cit., Vol. V, 671. see also, Paul Tillich, op. cit., 128.

but he further expounds the sacrament which is seven in number.[48] Faith and the sacraments are never dissociated. Even in infants, the children believe through others, as through others they contract those sins which are washed out in baptism. The sacraments are things of the senses: and without them the religion is not Christian. Thus, Aquinas Sacraments are necessary according to Augustine not only for baptism but for others also. The sacraments are needed for Salvation.

## C. Church

Augustine·Doctrine of the Church has a great influence on all the Christian Churches. The being of the Church is not found in personal character of Christian in it but the union of the whole Churches with Christ. The Church is not made of saints as the Donatists held but a mixed body of saints and repented sinners.[49] Augustine employed the Universal concept of the Church, that is mystical in nature. He views the Church as Universal Catholic Church, with its hierarchy and sacraments and with its centre at Rome.[50] He talked about the visible and invisible Church. He says Church is the mixed society, both of good and bad. He says Church in the present day is like a pilgrimage and it contains and is mother of all.

In the same line, **Aquinas** also seems to be speaking and says Rome is the mistress and mother of all the Churches. To obey her is to obey Christ. This is according to decision of the Holy Councils and the Holy Fathers. The unity of the Church presupposes a supreme centre of authority. To the Pope, it belongs to determine what is faith and subjection to Her is necessary for Salvation.[51] Aquinas said heresy is crime and if some entered Church and became heretic, he must if necessary, be forced by violent measures to obey the faith.

---

48 The seven sacraments correspond to seven cardinals and seven mortal sins. They are remedies of sin, and make for the perfecting of man in the righteousness.

49 Warren Thomas Smith, "Augustine of Hippo", In Mircea Eliad ed., *The Encyclopedia of Religion*, Vol. I, (New York: Macmillan Pub. Com., 1987), 523.

50 J. N. D. Kelly, *Early Christian Doctrines* (New York: Harper & Brothers, 1960), 413.

51 Philip Schaff, op. cit., Vol. V, 674.

Well he bases himself on Augustine but moves out on the issue of authority and gives full power to Pope.

## D. Grace of God

Augustine understood grace as the liberating force, which sets human nature free from itself incurred bondage of sin. He also understood grace as the healer of human nature. So, grace is absolutely necessary to Christian virtue. It is necessary for every good work, for every good thought and for every good word of man at every moment. It is moreover, unmerited. So a man without grace can do nothing good, this grace works progressively or by degree which removes all the consequences of fall. This is given by God to a certain number of people who can't be augmented or diminished, they belong to him eternally.

In the same line even Thomas speaks and quotes 1 Cor. 12:3, "every truth, by whoever spoken is from the Holy Ghost". Thomas says we can't know truth without grace. Human mind can know the Divine light through grace only. Thus, truth can be known only by the help of grace and not man by himself (Summa Theologica I-II, 109, I).[52] Man can't will and do well without grace. In the corrupted state man needs grace so that he may be healed and may be able to carry out the good works. Man can't merit eternal life without grace. Man by natural powers, can't produce meritorious works proportioned to eternal life, but for this high power he needs the power of grace. So, without grace man can't have eternal life (Summa Theologica I-II, 109, 5).[53] Thus, man without grace can't rise from sin. For sin is transient as to the act and abiding in its guilt. Rising from sin means that man has restored to him what he lost by sinning. Thus, God through grace only restores (Summa Theologica I-II, 109, 7)[54] Thus, on the issues of grace Thomas in general sense seems to depend upon Augustine and speak of the similar thoughts.

52 Anton C. Pegis, op. cit., 652.

53 Ibid., 660.

54 Ibid., 664.

## E. Free Will

Augustine says God created human with free will to choose between good and evil. By choosing evil they lost their free will and therefore needed God's grace to be saved and to live righteously.[55] Man does things not out of necessity but as a matter of freedom. Human free will has been weakened but not eliminated or destroyed through sin. In order that free will to be restored and healed it requires the operation of Divine grace. Augustine even says the human free will really exists in sinners, but that is compressed by sin.

According to Thomas, man possesses faculty of the free will as something distinct from reason. Free will makes the choice. Free will is the faculty which enables us to follow any one of the roads opened up by the intellect. Free will needs the grace of God to incline it to right choice. It was the abuse of free will that Adam lost his integrity, his freedom from fault. Free will is nothing else than the power of choice, which is the faculty of will. When the will becomes slave of Jesus Christ it can choose the will of God and it can also choose things which are good.[56] Thus, Thomas sees liberty as: liberty as regard an act (in that the will is free to act or not to act); liberty as regard the object (in that it can will this or its contrary); and liberty as regards the end (in that it can will good or evil). Man is free to choose the best.[57] Thus, Thomas thought builds upon Augustine and he only takes reason ahead and attaches to intellect.

## F. Predestination

Predestination in general is a necessary attribute of Divine will. The Greek Fathers and Tertullian, Ambrose, Jerome and Pelagius taught about a conditional predestination which was dependent on the free act of man. But, Augustine taught an unconditional election of grace, and restricted the purpose of redemption to a definite circle of

---

55 C.T. McIntire, "Free will and Predestination Christian Concepts", *in the Encyclopedia of Religion*, edited by Mircea Eliade , Vol.V (New York: Macmillan Pub. Company, 1987), 427.

56 W. B. Monahan, op. cit., 210-214.

57 Etienne Gilson, *The Spirit of mediaeval Philosophy*, translated by A. H. C. Downes (New York: Charles Scribner's Sons, 1940), 318-319.

the elect, who constitute the minority of the race. God has resolved from eternity to reveal some of His grace by rescuing them from the mass of perdition. This is the election of grace and God determines and knows what he will do. The predestination thus has reference to good only not evil. He takes passages from Romans 9 chapter and I Tim.2: 4.[58] Thomas develops his concept of predestination from the Divine providence as the starting point. The elects are substituted for the angels who lost their first estate, even as the Gentiles were substituted for the Jews. The number of the elect is unknown, but they are the minority of the race. God's loves all men. He leaves men to themselves and those who are lost, are lost by their own guilt. Thus, the doctrine is derived from Augustine in purer sense.

## G. Idea of God

Augustine's idea of love is the power which unites the mystical and ethical elements in his idea of God. He is more interested in the unity of God than indifferent *hypostasis*, the three person in God. He takes with uttermost seriousness the full quality of the three Divine persons, who differ only in their mutual relations. He starts not with the Father as the fount of Godhead but with God himself who speaks of essence rather than substance. He rejects any suggestions that there is one essence of Godhead and the three persons exits on different level.[59] On the relation of God to the World, Augustine spoke of Doctrine of Creation out of nothing. The World in no moment is independent of God. To Augustine, being was eternal immutability.

Thomas Aquinas understood God as being whose nature it is to be such an existential act. He says that essence of God is his *esse "to be"*. In human experience a "being", is something that is or exits. In God there is nothing to which existence can be attributed. He uses the analogy to know God and we know God in respect to Universe.[60] Thomas says God can be known by argument from motion, nature of efficient cause, possibility of necessity, gradation in things, and

58 Philip Schaff, op. cit., Vol. III, 851-855.

59 D. F. Wright, "Augustine", in *the Dictionary of Theology*, edited by Ferguson & D. F. Wright (England: IVP, 1988), 60.

60 Etienne Gilson, *History of Christian Philosophy in the Middle Ages* (London: Sheed and Ward, 1955), 368-369.

the governance of the World. Thomas says unity of equality and of substance is lost in the procession.

Augustine equates **Spirit** with gift and love. As the bond of communion between the Father and the Son, the Spirit is their mutual love as well as gift that unites God's people. He gives the analogy for Trinity as memory, intelligence and will. Since God is person, and that means a unity, all acts of God towards the outside are acts of the whole Trinity, even the act of incarnation.[61] For Thomas, Holy Spirit is union of what differentiates Father and Son. The Spirit has the dual role in the theology of Thomas. His is the procession of will or love. Love is the force impelling to unity, but it also carries the subject out of himself and is an endeavor to attain union beyond possession already given in knowledge. So, God the Spirit is God, both as perfectly united and resting in himself in love, and translated ecstatically out of himself by love. The second role of the Spirit is that Spirit is the medium of the gracious indwelling of the Trinity and so he is the person to whom the gift is appropriated. The Holy Spirit is called Spirit the general name for God, because he is what is common to Father and Son.[62]

For Augustine the **concept of atonement** is redemption from the bondage of Satan. He says Christ blood was the price paid for us to devil which he accepted. So, atonement for Augustine was to bring reconciliation and restoration. The essence of atonement lies in the expiatory sacrifice offered for us by Christ. He adopts the Anselmic view of the atonement.[63] The infinitude of human guilt makes it fitting that the Son of God should make atonement. Thomas takes up all the main data of Christ's life, from the conception to crucifixion. Justification is not a progressive process, but a single

61 D. F. Wright, op. cit., 61.

62 W. J. Hankey, op. cit., 121-122.

63 Tony Lane, op. cit., 61. Anselm held the satisfactory theory. He says that sin has robbed God what should be given to him. Sin creates contractual debt. So a satisfaction should be there and what ever is taken from God should be given back. Our sin has infinity gravity. Therefore human owe God an infinite satisfaction, but due to loss of original righteous it is impossible. Thus Christ was man and infinite as Christ being God. His death on the cross overcame the devil. Thus in Christ for human satisfaction is there for their debt. The whole Trinity is involved in the transaction.

instantaneous act. Thus, God is never changing. It was the change in man that rendered the incarnation necessary. The incarnation is God's communion of His goodness to man: the union is of the divine word with the soul and flesh of man. The incarnation surpasses the power of reason.[64]

## H. Idea of Scripture

For Augustine, Scriptures were sacred and was the Word of God. He believed that the Bible was divinely inspired which was a holy tradition. Holy Scriptures were the work of God's finger because they have been completed by the operation of the Holy Ghost. Same idea is of the Thomas. He says if the authority of the Holy Scripture be allowed to suffer in the slightest degree, our faith loses its stability. Holy Scripture affirm the authority of God and speaks of the Incarnation of Christ. Thus, the Scriptures should be held very highly.

## Conclusion

Augustine can be called the Pillar of Christian faith who time and again defended the faith and stood with the Church. His thought have become the stepping stone for the Middle Ages and still he is living in the modern theological circle scenario. Augustine was not only a theologian but great spiritual master. Augustine is one who teaches us both through his writings as well as through his life. Augustine authority has never been challenge fully. Even Thomas Aquinas for his synthesis uses Augustine in many areas as his basis. Marrou Henry says Augustine was used by almost all the theologians in one or the other way.[65] He ruled the entire theology of the Middle Ages. Anselm, Thomas Aquinas and Bonaventura are nearly affiliated to him. No other persons than Augustine has put the permanent effects on people. Augustine contributed much to the development of the doctrinal basis which Catholicism and Protestantism hold together.

---

64 W. B. Monahan, op. cit., 145.

65 Marrou Henry, *Men of Wisdom: St Augustine and his influence through the Ages* (London: Longmans, n.d), 164.

Augustine can be called the first forerunner of the Reformation because he first gave light on the doctrine of sin and grace. Augustine was held in so Universal esteem that he could exert influence in all directions. In the same direction Thomas Aquinas takes from in many ways. His source would be Aristotle concepts and as well Augustine. Aquinas also occupies a high place as the member of the company of the eminent Churchmen of all ages. Thomas was scriptural and truly Catholic. Thus, Aquinas differs from Augustine because of the need of the time and thus he should be appreciated not criticized as some of the Evangelical reformers criticized.

Chapter III

# Historical Models of Jesus' Death (Atonement)

## Introduction

The English word atonement is derived from the words, 'at-one-ment', to make the two parties at one, to reconcile two parties, one to another. It means essentially reconciliation. In current usages it means, the process by which the obstacles to reconciliation are removed. The phrase 'to atone for' means the undertaking of a course of action designed to undo the consequences of a wrong act with a view to the restoration of the relationship broken by the wrong act.[66] The word atonement originally meant simply reconciliation. **F. W. Dillistone** says "The concept of atonement denoted the means, an act or a payment, through which harmony was restored".[67] In

66 James Atkinson, "Atonement," in *A Dictionary of Christian Theology*, edited by Alan Richardson (London: SCM Press, 1969), 18.

67 F. W. Dillistone, "Atonment," in *A New Dictionary of Christian Theology*, edited by Alan Richardson & John Bowdon (London: SCM Press, 1983), 50.

Biblical context to speak more precisely, it means the work of Christ culminating at Calvary. In Old Testament the phrase, 'to make atonement' frequently occurs in ceremonial context which denotes an action or serial of actions by means of which guilt could be removed.[68]

The term occurs often in the KJV of Old Testament as the rendering of Hebrew word root *Kaphar/ Kippur* meaning covering but in New Testament once (Rom.5:11). The word atonement doesn't appear in the modern English Version of New Testament at all.[69] **D. M. Baillie** says, "it is from the sacrificial system of ancient Israel that we have inherited the whole terminology of atonement, expiation, propitiation, reconciliation; it seems to me that after a long puzzling story we find that the system reaching in the Christianity of New Testament a climax in which it is completely transformed into the idea of an atonement in which God alone bears the cost".[70]

Even though the word is not there but the idea is expressed in many forms. The death of Jesus is the framework of interpretation. The Testimony of New Testament writers is that Jesus died on a Cross. Broadly speaking there are two basic objectives seen in Bible about Jesus' Mission. First, to remove the curse that has come on humankind by disobedience and second to restore the estranged relationship between God and Humankind. So, His Sacrifice expiates the sins of human beings and He reconciles humankind to God on the Cross (1Cor.5:7, Heb.7:27, Phil2:7-9). The question is raised how could God allow His chosen to be treated like this? Paul gives answer to this by stating that, "Messiah died for our sins..." (1Cor.15:3). The Phrase 'for our sin' have proved capable of many interpretations and these during the time have expanded into which is called theories of atonement. Every theory tries to see the particular event of the death of the Messiah.[71] This chapter tries to deal with an

68 F. W. Dillistone, "Atonment," in *A New Dictionary of Christian Theology*, edited by Alan Richardson & John Bowdon (London: SCM Press, 1983).

69 James Atkinson, op. cit., 18.

70 D. M. Baillie, *God was In Christ: An Essay on Incarnation and Atonement* (London: Faber and Faber Ltd., 1961), 175.

71 F. W. Dillistone, op. cit., 50-51.

appraisal of some of the traditional theories or models of Jesus' death in order to understand Christ's atoning work.

## Traditional Models or Theories of Atonement

The various theological theories in which the Church has expressed its theology of atonement are quite simple. The theories are the various answers made by theologians in different ages to the question: How did Christ effect this great change in human's relation to God of which Christian life and faith are evidence?

### A. Ransom Theory/Model

Ransom theory was based on the assumption that it was Satan who stood in the way of human's redemption and that he could be bought of only by the payment of a ransom price such as the death of Christ.[72] So, suffering and death of Jesus Christ was the paid price for the redemption of the fallen human being because of sin. The theory is developed basing on the scriptural references such as Mk. 10: 45; 1 Pet.1: 18-19 where the idea of redeeming or purchasing by the blood of Jesus Christ is seen. As the religious situation was changing such attempts were made and forced Christian writers with the necessity of theorizing about the atonement in way that was not done before. The Gnostic theology forced the Church into the development of this thought of atonement to reply the heretical objections. Religion of Gnostics was somewhat a religion of redemption in mystic sense. If the Church was to hold it own thought against them, then it required to have a perfect scheme of redemption. It had to explain why a God of love should not forgive sin without demanding the death of His Divine Son.[73]

**Irenaeus** (ca. 140-202) is believed to be the first writer who definitely conceived the idea of dogmatic theology as distinct from an apologetic Philosophy. He is believed to be the pioneer who developed the theory of atonement. He started his articulation in

---

72 Albert C. Knudson, *The Doctrine of Redemption* (New York: Abingdon-Cokesbury Press, 1933), 357.

73 Hastings Rashdall, *The Idea of Atonement In Christian Theology* (London: MacMillan and Co., 1920), 234-235.

realizing the fact that the World is in need of an assurance of victory over arch enemies- sin, death and devil. He showed the death of Jesus as the sacrifice made for the whole humanity whereby caused the victory for the humans over their enemies. In order to develop the doctrine of atonement he uses the work of Christ as representative one: he uses the David Goliath model of representation where the victory of the nation was solely determined by their individual representation.[74] So the destiny of total race of humankind has been centered in its own protagonists- first Adam and then Jesus Christ. Irenaeus also demonstrates the indispensable relation between the Incarnation and the Atonement, for Christ would have not truly redeemed us by His blood if He had not been truly made man.

Later, **Athanasius** (ca. 296-373) advocated the Ransom theory. According to him, the turning away of human from God resulted in their coming under the dominion of death and corruption. He sees the atonement as the development of that which our Lord took upon himself at the incarnation through which the Eternal Word entered the human situation. He believed that the death of Jesus on the Cross is the ransom, due of human, through which the middle wall of partition between God and human was broken down, it reconciled the World to God. This was necessary in order to secure God's faithfulness; mere forgiveness would have not secured this not restored human nature from corruption.[75]

Later, **Gregory of Nyssa** (ca. 335-395) followed the thought of ransom and developed it. According to him, the jealousy of devil to devour the goodness of Jesus was deceived by the Eternal Word concealed within human flesh. He says, "It was that God, in order to make himself easily accessible to him who sought the ransom for us, veiled himself in our nature. In that way, as it is with greedy fish, he might swallow the Godhead like a fishhook along with the flesh, which was the bait".[76] The Gregory of Nyssa's theory of ransom

---

74 Robert S. Paul, *The Atonement and the Sacraments* (New York: Abingdon Press, 1960), 48.

75 L. W. Grensted, *The Atonement in History and in Life: A Volume of Essays* (London: SPCK, 1929), 181-182.

76 Robert S. Paul, *The Atonement and the Sacraments,* op. cit., 54-55. See also L. W. Grensted, 183.

was attacked by **Gregory of Nazianzus** (ca. 329-389) by asking the question that the ransom was paid to whom? Was the ransom paid to the evil one? Was it paid to God the Father? If so could the Father delight in the blood of His Son? With the realization of difficulty in finding the answer, Gregory of Nazianzus took up the representative character of Christ's work and stressed the obedience of Christ. Christ became New Adam to take place of the old, just so he makes my disobedience his own as the head of the whole body.[77] **Augustine** (ca. 354-430) rejected any idea of the death of Christ appeasing the wrath of God, but he said that the human race had been delivered into the power of the Devil by the justice of God when Adam sinned. But this did not remove human from God's grace and power, and human's sins delivered them to devil, so the remission of sins in Christ frees them from devil's power. Augustine viewed that when devil slew Christ, he took something that did not belong to him.[78]

## An Appraisal

The Ransom theory undoubtedly dominated in the Christian doctrine of atonement through the centuries but there is no clear cut answer that to whom the ransom price was paid in real sense. Basil of Caesarea, Origen, Ambrose and Jerome held the view that ransom was paid to the devil by referring Paul's statement that we were 'bought at a price' (1Cor. 6:20, 7:23).[79] The theory is inadequate in its articulation because it leaves the question unanswered. If the ransom price was paid to devil then the very idea of sovereignty of God comes under serious question because it gives devil the dominion and power. It would even more difficult to think gracious God demanding the Blood of His Son. The classical theory had been criticized by Enlightenment Theologians for not being objective theory. They considered it as relic of Judaism surviving in Christianity. Thus, it had begun the talk of subjective and objective

---

77 Robert S. Paul, *The Atonement and the Sacraments,* op. cit., 54-55. See also L. W. Grensted, 57.

78 Ibid., 60.

79 L. W. Grensted, op. cit., 185.

views of atonement.[80] The classical theory of ransom also bring the exclusive element that only Jesus Christ has been atoned for us brushing aside others religious ways. It is also seen that dualism was not common in liberal Protestant theology of 18th and 19th centuries, but the classical idea of atonement is dualistic in nature. If dualism is eliminated it is impossible to go on thinking of existence of powers hostile to God. Thus, from Enlightenment time to 19th century lay under the influence of idealistic metaphysics and was monistic.[81]

## B. Satisfaction Model/The Judicial Model

This Theory is associated with **Anselm** (ca. 1033-1109) who holds that Jesus' death on Cross offered a satisfaction to God for the sins of human. The word satisfaction is in origin a Roman legal term signifying the discharge of an obligation, but it was restricted to those cases in which discharge was affected by some means. It first entered theology in the works of Tertullian (circa 200) who used it of penance for sins.[82] Anselm' major contribution for this came from his book, '*Cur Deus Homo*?' The book is, in the form of dialogue between him and his disciple named Boso to whose questions he answers. He argued strongly against the long prevalent view that Christ's death was a ransom paid to the devil, the price demanded to release human form Satan who held human being in his grip. He took the view that ransom was paid not to the devil but to God, whose pure majesty had been outraged by the sin of human being His creature. The Judicial view means essentially that Jesus Christ, as man, bore the penalty of human sin and offered satisfaction for it in our stead.[83]

Because of sin, human being were left with the necessity to either satisfy God or to receive punishment. Since the sin of human was against infinite God, it demanded an infinite satisfaction. Human being could not give this satisfaction and thus, Christ rendered to God

80 Gustav Aulen, *Christus Victor: An Historical Study of the Three Main Types of the idea of Atonement* (London: SPCK, 1931), 23-24.

81 Ibid., 27.

82 William E. Wilson, *The Problem of the Cross: A Study of the New Testament Teaching* (London: James Clark & Co., limited, 1929), 15.

83 James Atkinson, op. cit., 23.

this satisfaction. He was a human and so it came from human's side. He was sinless and thus he was able to give God what he required. As He is God and infinite he gave an infinite satisfaction in order to compensate for the sin of human.[84]

## An Appraisal

Some positive thought can be noted about this model. Anselm insists that human's sin is against God which is right. Moreover, to that he views that human being can't save themselves which also sounds true. In accordance with the penitential system of the medieval Church the theory assumes that a third party can give satisfaction for the damages caused to God's reputation. But, the theory doesn't show explicitly as to how the death of Christ affects the Salvation of human being. Anselm theory seems to be not fully true because when he says sins of human being is sin against infinite being and it is an infinite sin and requires a infinite satisfaction. The logic is how can a tiny creature like human being do any injury to an infinite God? One of Anselm's most difficult problems is to reconcile his theory with the mercy and forgiveness of God. Anselm maintains that for God to forgive human being, the satisfaction that is due to Him is simple that human being can't pay the debt is to say that God merely remits when he has no chance of receiving, and this makes a mockery of the forgiveness of God. This theory didn't give any importance to the dimension of human being one with Christ and his death and resurrection. But, if we understand Anselm intention rightly it was not simply to destroy the ancient theory as such, but to re-establish the doctrine of atonement upon a firmer basis.

## C. Moral Influence Model/Exemplary Model

This theory is associated with **Peter Abelard** (ca. 1079-1142). This theory is also called subjective theory or the exemplarist theory which counters the idea found in former theories. The moralist considers the idea of the transfer of punishment and excessive emphasis on the outward suffering of Christ that was found unnecessary in other theories. The older theories give an idea that mercy can be

84 William E. Wilson, op. cit., 16.

purchased.[85] Abelard attacked the imagery of classical idea of the atonement and its dualistic outlook as well as Anselm theory. On one hand, he refused to allow the idea of the atonement to be connected in any way with devil; on the other hand, he sought to prove the impossibility of the idea of satisfaction, for if Adam's lesser fault required such a satisfaction, how much greater ought to be the satisfaction demanded by sins against Christ. He emphasized that Christ is a great teacher and example, who arouses responsive love in human; this love is the basis on which reconciliation and forgiveness rests.[86]

So, for Abelard the suffering of Christ was supreme example. Christ brought the message of Divine forgiveness and His whole life revealed the love of God in a way which stirs human being's heart for fresh repentance.[87] The moral influence theory held that the Cross is the expression of God's love and that the death of Jesus Christ and human response to it constitutes in themselves atonement. The idea is that Cross does not in itself change the relation between God and human beings rather the effect of Cross have to be located in the consciousness of believers. Thus, this theory implies that atonement should become subjective to every believer. R. S. Franks maintained that it is more a religious than moral theory since it had to do primarily with Divine grace demonstrated to us by God's love in Jesus Christ and in our response to that grace.[88]

## An Appraisal

This theory has come under severe criticism that it does not take into account the seriousness of sin rather it emphasizes on the change of humans mental and spiritual attitude. Thus, the idea of sin in this theory is superficial and intellectual and its cure also is intellectual through the perception of the love of God in Christ. The question is raised if Christ work only symbolizes or signifies the love of God,

85 Thomas Hywel Hughes, *The Atonement: Modern Theories of the Doctrine* (London: George Allen & Unwin Ltd., 1949), 200-201.

86 Gustav Aulen, op. cit., 112.

87 James Atkinson, "Atonement," *A Dictionary of Christian Theology,* op. cit., 23.

88 Robert S. Paul, *The Atonement and the Sacraments,* op. cit., 82.

it shows only what the OT had already taught. It also notes that just moral influence of Jesus' death would not release people from the power and enslavement of sin in biblical sense. Robert S. Paul states that, "Abelard is the persecuted hero.... Love is the theme, even though a closer reading of the facts reveals that the hero (Abelard) was no saint and that the love had more to do with *eros* than with agape". [89] When a person is conscious of his own sin, knows he can't perform without the assistance of a power that is greater than his own, the moral theory becomes meaningless unless a person is given the assurance that God makes him available His resources. In the New Testament God is seen as the agent in every aspect of atonement. It is Godward, rather than humanward side that receive the emphasis. God initiates the movement of redemption; His will is the power which brought reconciliation. But this movement is seen in opposite direction in the moral influence theory. Here the movement is human ward which shows that human initiates the process of redemption through their response to the suffering of the Cross.[90]

This model gives us the key to Cross. Not it is Godward or Satanward but it is Humanward side the all important thing. The orthodox thought had found it hard to accept and so it was condemned. Later in the 19th century this concept with its conception of Christ's death as the supreme revelation of the Divine love was revived by Schleiermacher and Ritschl and has gained its momentum. Thus, it brings the atonement from an ethical interpretation.[91]

## D. The Penal Model

This model was basically advocated by reformers. It has been said that **Martin Luther** (1483-1546) formulated the Penal theory. We find that Luther was highly influenced by Augustine thought and thus his theology is built on his frame work. The model holds that the death of Jesus Christ is the penalty caused by human sin. There is therefore no need of priestly absolution, nor of good works nor of

89 Robert S. Paul, op. cit., 81.

90 Thomas Hywel Hughes, op. cit., 204-205.

91 Albert C. Knudson, op. cit., 372.

any human action but only of faith.[92] The development of this penal conception arose from the idea that the death of Jesus Christ and His enduring suffering as the satisfaction to the justice and honour of God. Luther's idea of this is found in his commentary on St. Paul's Epistle to Galatians where he declared that the death of Christ is the penalty bore by him as a result of our sin.[93] Grensted Quotes Luther, "whatever sins you and we, all have done, and shall for the future do, belong to Christ as if He himself has done them".[94] Thus, this model speaks of God as God of justice and human are at fault and are to be penalized. But, Christ comes into the picture and stead of us he takes our, punishment thereby we the sinner are acquitted.

## An Appraisal

It should not be forgotten that the Lutheran and even Augustinian doctrine of fall and the Divine remedy for the fall imply literal truth of the Old Testament story concerning the origin of the human race, the sin of Adam and penalty imposed upon them and many other narratives without being really contained in it. In the modern time, the whole concept of infallibility has been dimmed and thus, we need to look from this framework the whole things. Thus, we need to ask the question that is this kind of model really viable now in the post-model thinking. The theory is also inconsistent with the Christian ethic which sums up the whole moral law in the requirement of Universal love and love being the most adequate expression of Character of God. In this theory, we find the opposition between God's justice and God's love whereby implying the idea of dualism in the nature of God. Thus, its emphasis on justice of God leaves human with no right, which shows the seriousness of punishment of sin rather than the restoration of the sinners. As we speak in its logical form, the penal theory seems mechanical, external, and almost immoral, for it makes no demand for any ethical change in humans.

92 L. W. Grensted, op. cit., 214.

93 Robert S. Paul, op. cit. 92-93.

94 L. W. Grensted, op. cit., 215.

## E. The Classic or Dramatic Model of Atonement (Conflict-Victory)

The Concept of '*Christus Victor*' which is advocated by Bishop **Gustaf Aulen (1879-)** as being the truly classical view shows that Christ did battle with devil and defeated him once and for all. Thus, atonement is, from start to finish, the costly but victorious conflict of God himself, in Christ, with the forces of evil.[95] This is a cosmic warfare against a very real enemy, and it involves Divine self sacrifice, but it is thereby triumphant over evil, with an eternal victory which is ever present. Here, the stress is on incarnation as a whole and the resurrection of Jesus is seen as the manifestation of the victory over the evil power on the cross.

So Christ's life, death and resurrection all are understood as aspects of the Divine struggle with evil power. This theory ensures the important sense that atonement is throughout God's work and not ours and that God's purpose of love was to reconcile the world to himself. Christ's work was mighty victory: we share His cross but with the hope of resurrection. D. M. Baillie says, "The objective work can't be separated from its subjective aspect by which atonement becomes a reality in the hearts and lives of human being. And this happens above all through the story of Cross of Christ, the point in human history where we find the actual outcropping of the Divine atonement. This is what brings individuality back to God".[96]

## Conclusion

With this examination of various theories of atonement it is clear that one theory can't stand isolate from the other. At the same time, it is also obvious that there can't be a single complete and final model of the atonement: because there are depths in God that we can't fathom since they are beyond the capacity of the finite mind. One thing all model shows that the Cross is the supreme demonstration of God's love for human kind. I think this can be the decisive factor for us to consider the atonement concept. The whole question is that what difference death of Jesus makes to the World? In this regard we can't

95 D. M. Baillie, op. cit., 200.

96 Ibid., 200-201.

answer speculative questions as to what might have been what God might or might not have done. But, we can say about atonement that it not only gives us the Christian view of God but also shows his mercy which is for whole cosmos. So, incarnate Jesus is what gives us liberation which leads us to new life.

Chapter IV

# Contemporary Models of Universal Significance of the Christ-Event

## Introduction

Christology has been and continues to be an area of central concern in Christian living. It embraces the person and work of Jesus and the meaning persons find in Him. The meaning suggests personal commitment, calls for transforming action, affirms Kingdom values, proclaims a vision of life for this world and the next, and takes shape in ecclesial communities that witness the presence of God in the history of the cosmos. The greatest challenge of our day is that: How a Christian should understand who Jesus Christ, in the context of world religion? Is the life and work of Jesus Christ Universally significant? What are the paradigms for understanding this Christ event and its relevance for the whole cosmos? This chapter highlights some of the paradigms and Asian thinking of Christ event in relation to resurrection.

## What is Christ-event?

Christian thought is basically centered around the life and work of Jesus Christ. This begins with the self revelation of God in the person of Jesus which forms an event in history. He becomes the one who is proclaimed and the manifested one; the crucified one, and the risen one. The New Testament bears witness to the whole history of the Jesus as a person. So the whole person and work of Jesus Christ forms a Christ-event and are related to the symbols of cross-resurrection – incarnation.[97] Since, the Christ event includes the whole person and work of Christ; his personality, life and teaching, the response of loyalty he awakened, his death and resurrection, the receiving of the Spirit has a wider significance.[98] So, this Christ event can't be limited to some people or some geographical settings but it is an event which affects the whole humankind.

## Different Paradigms for the Universal Significance of Christ-event

In contemporary theology there are spectrums of views regarding the interpretation of the resurrection of Jesus. Generally people locate this variety of interpretation into three broader sections: firstly, there are theologians who hold the view that Jesus resurrection was a historical event of the past to which people have access primarily by the exercise of historical reason. Secondly, there are theologians who are more pessimistic about the whole of human reason and doubt its ability to support faith. This view denies speaking resurrection as an event of objective order. Thirdly, there are theologians who insist that the Easter faith of Christian is nothing more than a response based on historical life of Jesus from His birth to His death and not any post –mortem occurrence.[99] The story of resurrection is then held to be a way of expressing faith and it is the product of faith rather than

97 David Tracy, *The analogical Imagination: Christian Theology and the Cultural Pluralism* (London: SCM Press, 1981), 249.

98 John Macquarrie, *Jesus Christ in Modern Thought* (London: SCM Press, 1990), 22-23.

99 Peter Carnley, *The Structure of Resurrection Belief* (Oxford: Oxford Press, 1993), 9.

the ground of it, a myth rather than a fact. This section, I would like to concentrates on three paradigms which are Ecumenical paradigm, Historical paradigm and liberative paradigms. In the context of religious pluralism three models/paradigms are very much needed to understand the significance of Jesus Christ and even especially to understand the resurrection of Jesus.

## 1. The Ecumenical Paradigm

The development of a Christology in the context of religious pluralism is a major contribution of the Indian Church to theology. Due to its openness to other religions, without jettisoning the biblical faith, this Christology can be qualified as an ecumenical thought. The question which is precisely raised in connection with Christ event's Universal significance is: How we can understand the role and significance of Jesus Christ in the context of recognition of other religions? Is Jesus Christ superior to all others? The first plenary Council of the Catholic Church in India held in 1950 at Bangalore declared: "We acknowledge indeed that there is truth and goodness outside the Christian religion, for God has not left the nations without a witness to Himself, and the human soul is naturally drawn towards one true God".[100] S. J. Samartha points out that, "the possibility of the Spirit being present and active among those who are not baptized, and in communities outside the visible boundaries of the institutional Church, should be left open rather closed"[101]

## 2. The Historical Paradigm

Historical paradigm refers to the emphasis the authors have laid on the historical Jesus on the one hand and the impact of Jesus Christ on human history on the other. The historicity of Jesus Christ is indeed needed in the Indian context. Jesus Christ asserts the value and significance of the history. M. M. Thomas developed a Christ-

---

100 Jacob Kavunkal, SVD, "Indian Views on the Significance of Jesus Christ", in *What Does Jesus Christ Mean?* Edited by Errol D'Lima & Max Gonsalves (Bangalore: Dharmaram Publications, 2001), 66.

101 S. J. Samartha, "The Holy Spirit and People of other Faiths," in *To the Wind of the God's Spirit: Reflection on the Canberra Theme,* Comp., Emilio Castro (Geneva: WCC Publications, 1990), 56.

centered humanism in which the emphasis is on the contribution of human, "quest for a better quality of life and social justice".[102] He recognizes the presence of Christ in all struggles for justice, whether Christian or not. Similarly he discerns the presence of Christ in any spirituality whether Christian or not, that inspires the struggle for justice. Christ is present in these struggles as the cosmic Lord of history.[103] The Church responds to Christ's presence as Lord of history when it unites, with all adherents of all religions and secular ideologies in the Asian people's struggle to realize full humanity.[104]

In the same line of thought, S. J. Samartha also views the same concepts. He views that Christology today must stand at the point where these is concern of inter-religious dialogue and of struggle for just meet. Christology today has to take into account both the quest for a theology of religions and struggle for justice in society.[105] This meeting point one could identify as the work for the Kingdom of God because it is God's Kingdom, which is concerned not just with Christian and Christianity but with all our neighbors of other faiths, their hope and aspirations as well.[106] This thinking is primarily based on the incarnation, ministry & death, and resurrection of Jesus. Thus, Christ-event is relevant when historical and social concerns of any given context are interwoven.

The meaning of Christ event according to Samuel Rayan is: Poor in the present history are theological, Christological reality; the little ones, the least of Jesus' brothers and sisters, those who do the will of God (Mk.3:35) by hungering and thirsting for justice and

---

102 M. M. Thomas, *Towards a Theology of Contemporary Ecumenism* (Madras: CLS, 1978), 311.

103 M. M. Thomas, *Risking Christ for Christ's Sake* (Geneva: WCC Publications, 1987), 85.

104 M. M. Thomas, *Salvation and Humanization: Some Crucial Issues of the Theology of Mission in Contemporary India* (Madras: Christian Literature Society, 1971), 118.

105 S. J. Samartha, *One Christ Many Religions: Towards a Revised Christology* (New York, Maryknoll: Orbis Books, 1991), 135.

106 S. J. Samartha, *Courage for Dialogue* (New York, Maryknoll: Orbis Books, 1982), 114.

mercy on this Earth.[107] The oppressed and the poor are Jesus' vicar on Earth. To serve them is to serve Jesus. In their person, life, and struggles, God is present. It is this Jesus-experience and a committed participation in Jesus' struggle for justice and freedom that enabled the disciples to understand and to articulate Jesus' meaning and significance.[108] Rayan also asserts that, "Christ is in every starved man and deprived woman and hungry child; and in all the stripped, disposed and broken, regardless of what the compass says".[109] Jesus becomes present and relevant to all in this manner.

## 3. Resurrection of Jesus Christ: A liberative Paradigm

Under the liberative perspective, the views of Leonardo Boff, Jon Sobrino, and James H. Cone on resurrection will be discussed.

### A. Leonardo Boff

He viewed that the resurrection of Jesus constituted a great turning point of that community: only now did that profoundly understand who Jesus was and what he signified for the whole history of Salvation.[110] Jesus announced an absolute meaning to the world as a total liberation from all alienations that stigmatize human existence: from pain, from hatred, from sin, and finally from death as well. The resurrection rehabilitated Jesus before the world. It revealed that Jesus dies for the sins of the world. Resurrection came to reveal that Christ was not a bandit; neither abandoned by God, nor was a false prophet or a false messiah. By means of resurrection God rehabilitated him before the human race.[111] Resurrection of Jesus gives origin to the Church.

---

107 Samuel Rayan, "People's Theology", *Jeevadhara* 22 (1992), 196. Cited by Jacob Kavunkal, SVD, "Indian Views on the Significance of Jesus Christ", in *What Does Jesus Christ Mean?* Edited by Errol D'Lima & Max Gonsalves (Bangalore: Dharmaram Publications, 2001), 73.

108 Ibid., 197.

109 Samuel Rayan, "Worship in Spirit and Truth", *Jeevadhara* 23 (1993), 248.

110 Leonardo Boff, *Jesus Christ Liberator: A Critical Christology of our Time.* (Maryknoll: Orbis Books, 1978), 51.

111 Ibid., 130.

## Anthropological Relevance of Resurrection of Jesus

Boff says because of the resurrection of Jesus, Christianity is not a nostalgic religion that commemorates the past. It is the religion of the present that celebrates the certainty of living and personal presence. Christianity thus came to answer the most poignant problem of the human heart: What is to become of humankind? For the Christians, there is no longer utopia but only topia. The resurrection of Jesus seeks to be this utopia realized within the World, because resurrection signifies an eschatologization of human reality, an introduction of the human person, body and soul, into the Kingdom of God, total realization of the capacities God placed within human existence. With this, all the alienated elements that lacerated life have been annihilated, such as death, pain, hatred and sin. For the Christian, as of the moment of the resurrection there is no more utopia (In Greek: that which does not exist anywhere) but only topia (that which exists somewhere). Human hope was realized in Jesus resurrected and is already being realized in each person.[112]

## The Presence of Resurrected Jesus in Anonymous Christians

The resurrected Jesus is present and active in a special way in those who in the vast ambit of history and life carry forward his cause. This is independent of their ideological colorings or adhesion to some religion or Christian belief. Wherever people seek the good, justice, humanitarian love, solidarity, communion and understanding between people, wherever they dedicate themselves to overcoming their own egoism, making this World more human and fraternal, and opening themselves to the normative transcendent for their lives, there we can say, with all certainty, that the resurrected Jesus is present. It is because the cause for which he lived, suffered, was tried and executed is being carried forward. All those adhere to Jesus' cause are his brothers and sisters and he is acting in them so that there might be greater openness towards others and more human space of God.[113]

---

112 Leonardo Boff, *Jesus Christ Liberator: A Critical Christology of our Time*, (Maryknoll: Orbis Books, 1978), 135.

113 Ibid., 219.

This is in proper sense shows the Universal significance of Christ-event. Christ's resurrection brought new light for the vision of the World. It is the liberation of life from all its obstacles and conflicts in history. The resurrection unveils the life that was hidden in Jesus and that could not be devoured by the cross. It points to the goal and fulfillment sought by every liberation process. The resurrection of Crucified Jesus shows that it is not meaningless to die for other human beings. Jesus continues to exist among human beings, giving impetus to their struggle for liberation.

## B. Jon Sobrino

He views that Jesus' resurrection inaugurates a liberative future. It was understood to be the anticipation of a Universal resurrection. This means that we can't turn resurrection into nothing more than a past event. The risen one can't be turned into an origin myth that grounds the present.[114] The resurrection by its very nature, points towards the future of humanity. Thus, the essence of Christian faith can't be reduced to affirming the truth of past events. It must affirm what already is insofar as it has not yet been fulfilled for all.

The resurrection of Jesus speaks about humanity and history. God's action in Jesus has been a salvific action of pardon and revitalization rather that retribution. Humanity has been offered a new kind of life based on hope and love. Because Jesus rose from the dead as the 'firstborn of many brothers', we are pointed toward our own fulfillment and revitalization of history. We can and should live as new, risen human beings here and now in history.[115]

## Relevance of Jesus' Resurrection Today

One must have a radical hope for the future. One must possess a historical consciousness that sees history both as promise and as mission. And one must engage in a specific praxis that is nothing else but discipleship- the following of Jesus. The starting point of praxis should be love that concretizes Christian hope as a hoping against

---

114 Jon Sobrino S. J., *Christology at the Crossroads: A Latin American Approach* (Maryknoll: Orbis Books, 1978), 263.

115 Ibid., 377.

hope. The resurrection of Jesus is not one time event, something given once for all. Our horizon of understanding must be constantly fashioned anew. Our hope and praxis of love must be kept alive and operational at every moment. In this way, we can grasp the resurrection of Jesus.[116]

In the resurrection of Christ, the Spirit manifests itself as the power of God that is able to restore Christ to definite life. But, the Spirit also manifests itself in order to enable the disciples to grasp the objective of resurrection of Christ. The newness of Christ's resurrection is matched by something new in the disciples.[117] The resurrection of Christ is impossible unless it in turns launches history. The resurrection of Christ, the supreme symbol of victory over death and over the wretchedness of history is impossible provided we understand it in Christian way and not just an extraordinary wonder.[118]

## C. James H. Cone

Cone declares that God raised from the dead that is to say that our knowledge of Jesus is not limited to his life in Palestine. Jesus is not merely a historical person who once identified with the poor people of his land and subsequently was executed by the Roman authorities for disturbing the social and political status quo. The Crucified One is also the risen Lord. Faith in the resurrection means that the historical Jesus, in his liberating words and deeds for the poor, was God's breaking into human history, redeeming humanity from injustice and violence, and bestowing power upon little ones in their struggle for freedom[119]

## The Relevance of Resurrection

Cone says that black people's faith that Jesus was raised from the dead meant that his historicity and humanity are not the only

116 Jon Sobrino S J, *Christology at the Crossroads: A Latin American Approach* (Maryknoll: Orbis Books, 1978), 381.

117 Jon Sobrino S.J, The *True Church and the Poor* (Maryknoll: Orbis Books, 1984), 96.

118 Ibid., 87.

119 James H. Cone, *God of the Oppressed* (London: SPCK, 1977), 120.

relevant factors about his person. He is also the Divine one, who transcends the limitations of history by making himself present in our contemporary existence. This is the meaning of Jesus' resurrection.[120] It is within this context that the resurrection is political event.

The politics of the resurrection is found in its gift of freedom to the poor and the helpless. Being granted freedom while they are still poor, they can know that their poverty is a contrived phenomenon traceable to rich and is powerful in this world. This new knowledge about themselves and the World is through resurrection. Not to fight is to deny the freedom of the resurrection. It is to deny the reality of Christ's presence with us in the struggle to liberate the slaves from bondage. This is the political side of the resurrection of Jesus.[121] The affirmation 'Jesus is Lord', like the cry 'Christ is risen!' has political overtones. The Lordship of Christ emphasizes his present rule in the lives of the people, helping them to struggle for the maintenance of humanity in a situation of oppression.

C. S. Song summarizes the concept of resurrection by viewing that resurrection is the confession that our Redeemer lives. It is the testimony that although our skin can be destroyed, but with our flesh hat remains we can see God. Resurrection is the poem of freedom from prison bars. It is the song of victory after defeat in the struggle to be human. It is the hymn of life surrounded by death. Resurrection is the new space created by God for us in the World of toil, labor, pain and anguish. It is both inner and outer space of Salvation that is ours from God through Jesus. Theology is possible because of such space, both inner and outer. And it can be immensely enrich and deepen by the experience of such space in Asia.[122]

## Conclusion

The Christ-event undoubtedly has a Universal significance because the very life and work of Jesus Christ and the biblical witnesses clearly shows that Jesus Christ lived and died not for a particular people but for the whole humankind and the world. The Christ event is the

120 James H. Cone, *God of the Oppressed* (London: SPCK, 1977), 125.

121 Ibid.

122 Choan Seng Song, *Theology from the Womb of Asia*, (Maryknoll: Orbis Books, 1986), 206.

very act of God in the history of the World which has its impact on the whole cosmos. Christ is indeed the centre of our existence, centre of history, and centre of nature. Jesus Christ is Universally significant because in him a new mode of existence has began, a new Creation. Resurrection brings the freedom and new hope for the future that God would break all kinds of oppression and evil structures and vindicates all of as he was vindicated at resurrection. This is the power of resurrection that all will be resurrected first here from all traumas and then a hope to be with the resurrected Lord follows.

Chapter V

# Christology From Below: Need of the Hour

## Introduction

The word Christology is made up of two Greek words, *christos* and *logos*. *Christos* literally means anointed one, which in Hebrew means messiah. This means that the first part of Christology is influenced by Hebrew usage and second part is Greek. This Christology became the center of discussion which later was referred as Christological controversies. All this expression reflect the divinity and humanity of Jesus Christ and how this two can be one.[123] Thus, the origin of Christology seems most likely rooted in the understanding and background of Hellenistic and Judaist traditions. The Christological controversies refer exclusively to person or nature of Christ they refer on the one hand to the relation between his nature with that of God; on the on the other hand, to the relation which exits in Christ

123 Reginald H. Fuller & Pheme Perkins, *Who Is This Christ?* (Philadelphia: Fortress Press, 1983), 1.

himself between his Divine and his human nature.[124] My effort is to present the historical development of Christological conflict, and third, fourth and fifth century Christological approaches which will be followed by critical evaluation.

## I. Context or Background

In clarifying the nature of the faith several attempts were made during the second and third centuries that were rejected by the Church. Among these some referred the Son as one intimately related in dependence on the eternal God; some to God Himself in His relation to the World of nature; some to man like us who had the spirit of God working pre-eminently in him; and some to a prefect creature whom God brought into being before everything else. While such ideas where being promoted. There were people in the Church who criticized these ideas. These men handed down to later generations certain patterns of thinking which came to be regarded as the Church doctrine. Since, the thinking was not unified by second century there tradition almost began to develop: One of Alexandria, another in Antioch and third in the West.[125]

## Meaning of Christology from Below

The question about right order of doing things- Christology first or soteriology- was largely a protestant one. But, in the recent years debate in the Roman Catholic Church theology was of Christology from above or from below. Christology from above is the traditional modus operandi (mode of operation). One started with Christ as the eternal Son of God and second person of Trinity and moved from there to his incarnation and earthly life, then to his death, resurrection, and exaltation which has its justification in the prologue of John1:1-18 which precedes the history. Christology from below begins with the historical Jesus, and then works back to the question of his

124 Oscar Cullman, *The Christology of the New Testament* (Philadelphia: The Westminster Press, 1959), 3

125 V. C. Samuel, *The Council of Chalcedon Re-examined: A Historical an Theological Survey* (Madras: The Christian Literature Society, 1977), 3.

pre-existence and incarnation.[126] The disadvantage in Christology from above is that it tends towards docetism, apollinarianism or monophysitism. In other words, it does violence to Jesus' humanity in order to preserve his divinity at all costs. It is the humanity of Jesus which would give us impetus to do the theology for today. This conflict of above and below led to ecumenical discussions where efforts were made to bring solutions to the differences.

## II. Historical development of Christological Conflict

The problem of Christology, in the narrow sense of the word is to define the relation of the Divine and the human in Christ. This issue in fact can be fully seen in the fourth century where the whole argument moves around the *Nicaea* formulation (Son shared the same essence as of the Father). The most primitive confession has been, 'Jesus is Lord' which is seen from the apostolic age. [127] In first three centuries, the frontiers of orthodoxy were not so rigidly demarcated as they later became and important currents flowed outside the main channel which gave rise to some heretical trends.

In the second century **Firstly,** we find of Christology known as *Ebionism*[128], which had tried to deny the divinity altogether. The Ebionites were the offshoot of that specifically Jewish form of Christianity which was a great force in apostolic age. They rejected the virgin birth, regarding the Lord as a man normally born from Joseph and Mary, he was predestined Messiah and in this capacity he will return to reign on Earth.[129] **Secondly**, the concept of adoptionism which was basically of Theodoti and Artemas and by which Paul of Samosata was influenced has raised problem in sixties of the third centuries. He held that Christ was an ordinary man in nature, drawing a sharp distinction between the historical Jesus and the Word. Jesus Christ was one and Word was another, the former being from below

126 Reginald H. Fuller & Pheme Perkins, op. cit., 5-6.

127 J. N. D. Kelly, *Early Christian Doctrines* (London: Adam & Charles Black, 1958), 138.

128 Tertullian connects their name with one Ebion, the apocryphal founder for the sect, but in fact it derives from the Hebrew for poor which was a humble title everyone liked to be attached.

129 Kelly, op. cit., 139.

and latter from above. The relationship of the Word to Jesus Christ he described is of indwelling or participation. There is no question of Godhead being united to man in any concrete or substantial sense. Thus, he said Mary did not bear the Word, for Mary didn't exist before the ages; what she bore was a man equal to us, but superior in all things as a result of the Holy Spirit.[130]

**Thirdly** the Christological tendency which opposed Jesus' humanity was Docetism. They believed that Christ's manhood and suffering were unreal, phantasmal. Along with them was the idea of Gnosticism. The Gnostics believed that from the spiritual World of aeons, the Divine Christ descended and united himself for a time to the historical personage, Jesus; and accordingly later the body was formed, not out of ordinary flesh but of psychic substance. Christ Jesus was compounded of two distinct substance (*ousiai*) being the heavenly Christ and Jesus.[131]

## III. Christologies of Two schools- Antiochene and Alexandrian

The subsequent development of Christological thought is bound up with the divergent tendencies seen in two great schools of theology, the Antiochene and Alexandrian. The truths which these schools contended resulted in some great heresies such as Nestorianism and Eutychianism. They were on the one hand who led such stress on human nature of Jesus that they talked of Divine Logos dwelling in the man Jesus Christ; they seem to speak of two persons and two natures. These heresies were condemned at Council of Ephesus (431) and Chalcedon (451).

### A. Christology of Antiochene School (Logos Anthropos Christology)

This school was lead in opposition to Apolliniarism to lay special stress upon the reality and completeness of Christ's manhood, which insisted upon the distinction of the manhood from Godhead in one person. It wished to guard against the pantheistic tendency of the Alexandrain School to confuse the two natures, or to think of the

130 Kelly, op. cit., 140.

131 Ibid, 142.

Divine transforming into human. This led to its being conceived of as a separate personality, which resulted in Nestorianism, which so pressed the distinction as to separate the Persons. Some spoke, One person of Christ consist of two Sons, the Son of God and Son of Mary. They vindicated the historical Jesus, and pressed upon a real moral growth and development in Christ during his earthly life. So life of Christ according to this school was a continual progress, and every stage of this advance the Christ proved triumphant over all temptations, as a result of his union with Divine Logos.[132] They speak that essential union of human and the Divine are not here, nor there is an incarnation, but a moral union between the two natures. They speak of God as dwelling in Christ; the Logos assuming human nature, rather than of God becoming man or the Word made flesh.

The Antiochene School followed the inductive and rationalistic method, which consisted of careful examination of the facts of human nature and experience. They centered the attention upon the historical Christ; in its doctrine of inspiration it affirmed the immediate and historical reference of Scripture. It regarded the purpose of incarnation as the accomplishment of man's destiny rather than as a deliverance of him from the results of sin.[133] They see the vital connection between the doctrine of Christ's person and that of his redemptive work, and establish their Christology upon soteriological principles.

## B. The Alexandrian School

Alexandria was the special centre of Christological reflection in the Greek speaking world of the third century. The doctrine of Logos and the incarnation of this school occupied a central place led by Clement and Origen.[134] The Alexandrian school started from the Divine aspect of Christ's Person- the pre-incarnate Logos manifested in time and space through an incarnation which was a real revelation of God. In the Person of Christ it is not a man who is assumed, but

132 H. Maurice Relton, *A Study in Christology* (New York: The Macmillan Company, 1929), 20-21.

133 Ibid., 24-25.

134 Aloys Grillmeier, *Christ in Christian Tradition*, Vol. I (Oxford: Alden Press, 1965), 135.

the humanity is that of Logos, who was incarnate by the Holy Ghost of Virgin Mary and was made man.[135]

The unity in tension between the Logos and the flesh is main factor. It is true that clement has always been suspected of docetism but he consistently maintains the reality of human nature of Christ but his tendency to spiritualize make the reality of incarnation relative. Clement says the Logos has come from heaven; the Lord has entered into or attached Himself to, human flesh. He has created his own humanity.[136] Origen believed that the World of spiritual being including human souls pre-existed from all eternity; he applied this to incarnation. One of these souls, the one destined to be the souls of man Jesus, was from the beginning attached to the Logos with mystical devotion; it burned with love and desire for justice and became inseparably united with him.[137]

## IV. Ecumenical Decisions On Christological Controversies

Thus, from here we find, the Christological conflict began to rage on a large scale in the forth century. In the year 325 at Nicea the Church condemned the heresy of Arius who denied the deity of Christ. In the same century, at Constantinople in 381, the Church was obliged to express its disapproval of Apollinairs who didn't do justice to the truly human nature of Savor. In the fifth century, the Church began to reflect the relation of two natures and thus had to oppose the heresy of Nestorius and Eutyches in council of Chalcedon in 451. But, one thing should be noted here that these controversies were related to the full humanity of Christ. To all these councils and discussions Berkouwer calls the Ecumenical Decisions.[138]

### A. Nicean Council 325 A.D.

Before the beginning of the Arian strife, the Church appears to have reached three fixed truths in respect to Jesus as the fruits of the

135 H. Maurice Relton, op. cit., 24-25.

136 Kelly, op. cit., 153.

137 Ibid., 155.

138 G. C. Berkouwer, *Studies in Dogmatics: the Person of Christ* (Michigan: WM .B. Eerdmans Pub., Company, 1954), 59.

previous controversies. (a) The Sons unity of essence with the Father, (b) His eternal generation and (c) His personal distinction from the Father.[139] Suddenly the new conflicts broke out around the first and the second propositions which led for Nicean Council. The council of Nicea was mainly called to counter and reflect on the teachings of Arius[140] who held that, "God is eternal and one, there can't be anything beside Him that which is created and which has its origin in the Divine will. The Son is not co-eternal with the Father, but a created being, the Father was not always a Father, for there was a time when Son was not, yet created and hence God was not yet Father of His Son. The Son proceeds not from the being but from the will of the Father. He is not a true God but a creature; however, he is s perfect creature standing in very special relationship to God. The Son is inferior to Father and does not share in the being (homoousios-equal essence) of the Father."[141]

The whole council was dependent on the word homoousios (equal-essence). Arius was opting for the word (homoiousios - similar). At Nicea, Arius was condemned by the use of this word only. Jesus Christ is of one substance with the Father. The Greek word homoousios (of one substance) was the most controversial word in the creed. The creed of Nicea states, "We believe… in one Lord Jesus Christ, the Son of God, born of Father, the sole begotten; that is to say, of the substance of the Father, God from God, light from light, true God from true God, born not made, through all things were made, which are in heaven and on Earth…"[142] thus with this formulations Arius was condemned.

---

139 H.R. Mackintosh, *the Doctrine of the Person of Jesus Christ* (Edinburgh: T & T. Clark, 1912), 175.

140 Arius was a presbyter of Alexanderia and known for piety. Arius had his learning under the feet of Lucian of Antioch, a follower of Paul of Samosata. Lucian based his views on the Adoptianist chirstology of Paul of Samosata, who taught that Christ had been adopted by God as man. Like Origen he believed that Father is greater than Son but he didin't belive in the hierarchy of the Divine beings. In todays thought Arius teaching is found much in Jehovah Witness. The H.R. Mackintosh, op. cit., 176.

141 G. C. Berkouwer, op. cit., 60.

142 Philip Hughes, *The Church in Crisis: A History of the Twenty Great Councils* (London: Burns & Oates, 1961), 21.

## B. Apollinarianism

Apollinarianism controversy raised for the first time in an acute form the question of the complete humanity of Christ's Person. Apollinaris of Laodicea (died about 390) aimed to secure the complete unity of Christ's Person without sacrificing His real deity. He considered that Arians were right in objecting the doctrine of two natures. He said, "if perfect God were joined to perfect man, they would be two one, Son of God by nature, one by adoption."[143] The questions raised here are: How can the Logos assumed human nature in its completeness? If Christ was truly Divine could He be completely human? Was complete manhood compatible with sinless Godhead in One Christ?

Apollinaris found his starting point in a psychology which was Platonic in its origin & which was popular in Christian circle by the writings of Origen. Origen used Platonic tripartite division of human nature to explain the doctrine of pre-existence of soul. Origen had retained all these three: body, soul and spirit. Although Church rejected the doctrine of Origen of pre-existence of soul but the thought was present there. Apollinairs wanted to prove the sinlessness of Christ.[144] He took the starting point of three fold division of human nature: Body (soma), vital soul (sukhe) and rational or intellectual soul (nous) which was considered to be the seat of sinful instincts. He agreed with Arius that in Christ the Logos were united to a human body with a vital soul. But, he said that Logos united was not creature and not imperfect. The very fact Christ lacked a human nous, the seat of free will, free choice and mutability, secured his sinlessness.[145] He lacked a human nous and so he was not capable of sin. The place of human nous was taken by the Divine immutable and infallible Logos.

Two perfect natures seemed to him to involve a dual personality. The union of full divinity and full humanity in one person seemed to him to be an impossible amalgam. Thus, he sought to find an organic union between the two natures in an incarnation which resulted in

143 H. R. Mackintosh, op. cit., 198.

144 H. Maurice Relton, op. cit., 9.

145 Ibid.

the Creation of a new nature-divine human. In order to sought out the problem was to deny to Christ the possession of a human nous at all. This process led to the rejection of the personality of human nature, the most important constituent of man.[146] Apollinarianism was condemned at the council of Alexandria in 362 A.D.

## C. Council of Ephesus (431) – Nestorianism

In this controversy we find two people Nestorius[147] and Cyril of Alexandria. Nestorius while writing to Pope, Celestine I (422-432) said, "he says of the serious matter is the unconscious heresy of good Catholics and monks about the meaning of the belief that Christ is God. They are confused in their minds about the great mystery that Christ is both God and man, and they speak as though what is human in Christ was Divine. They talk that God was born, and being buried, and also invoke the most Holy Virgin Mary as the "God-bringing-forth, i.e., the mother of God-Theotokos. They should say she is Christotokos, the one who brought forth Christ, the mother of Christ. So the Virgin is Christotokos and not Theotokos."[148] In general we see he remained true to the Christological traditions of Antioch God the Word is distinguished from the man Jesus. The Holy Spirit didn't not create the Word, but formed a temple for him. Nestorius supported the total rejection of Theotokos and even asserted that Lord was mere man. He proposed the two nature concept of Christ.

But, Mr. Bethune Baker says, Nestorius was in reality no Nestorian. Since, he didn't hold the belief commonly attributed to him that in Jesus Christ two persons, person of a God and person of a man were mechanically joined together, which showed that there were two Sons and two Christ's. He didn't think of two distinctive persons joined together, but single person who combined in himself the two distinct things (substances), Godhead and manhood. He believed that no one should call Word of God a creature, or manhood

146 H. R. Mackintosh, op. cit., 11.

147 Nestorius, patriarch of Constantinople in 428, had received his education at Antioch. He was offended by the term *theotokos* which means mother of God. He suggested using *christotokos.*

148 Philip Hughes, op. cit., 37.

which was assumed incomplete.[149] In the council of Ephesus in 431 Nestorius was excommunicated.

## D. The Council of Chalcedon (451)

The council of Chalceon was called by emperor Marcion to resolve the affairs of Eutyches.[150] At Chalcedon both confusion and separation was rejected. The decision of Chalcedon was strongly influenced by the well known letter which Leo I addressed to Flavian in 449. In this letter he maintained that the two natures have its peculiar attributes. Thus, the Chalcedonian definition was born. "*One and only Son our Lord Jesus Christ, is perfect in Godhead and perfect in manhood, truly God and truly man, that he has a rational soul and a body. He is of one substance (homoousios) with the Father as God. He is like us in all things except sin. He was begotten of his Father before the ages as God but in these last days for our Salvation he was born of Mary the Virgin, the theotokos as man. This one and the same Christ, Son, Lord made known in two natures, without confusion, without change, without division and separation.*[151]

The definition makes four points in opposition to four ancient heresies: in Jesus Christ true deity (against Arius) and full humanity (against Apollinaris) are united in one person (Against Nestorius) and without being confused (against Eutyches). The Chalcedon definition

149 H. R. Mackintosh, op. cit., 204.

150 Eutyches belonged to the Alexandrian school of theology and eventually his Christology became docetic, Stressing the Divine nature of Christ as against the human nature of Christ. Held that in Christ the Divine and human natures were united to form a single nature or *Phusis*, and that this nature was Divine rather than human. He was one who said that the body of man became the boy of God, but the boy was human and the Lord incarnate was incarnate of the Virgin. He confessed that our Lord was of two natures (union of divinity and humanity in the incarnation), but after the union, one nature. Thus he spoke of two natures of Jesus before the union, but after the union and incarnation, he speaks not of two natures but of one nature. On this ground he was condemned by the synod of Constantinople in 348. V.C. Samuel, op.cit., xvii.

151 Tony Lane, *The Lion Book of Christian Thought*, (Tiruvalla: Suvartha Books, 1984), 37.

reasserts the unity of Christ's Person. The reality and permanence of each nature and relationship between the two natures.

## Critical Evaluation

If the Nicene formula safeguards the truth of Christ's essential divinity, the Chalcedonian definition equally safeguards the truth of his essential humanity. Both these truths are vital for any Christology which claims the New Testament and Christian tradition as its foundation. The main question arises which approach should be taken while developing the Christology. We have seen that that Chalcedonian definition states but does not solve the problem. The question remains same, i.e., in what way the definition can be interpreted? In an Alexandrian (above) or in an Antiochan (below) direction. The answer is both because they both contain the element of truth and they both should be taken this consideration. **John Sobrino** says, "The Christology should embrace all reality of both above and below lest it will result in forming wrong methodology."[152]

S. J. Samartha while developing a contextual theology explains the difficulty of above theology and calls for change in the thinking pattern. He says the theology from above does not do justice to the humanity of Jesus of Nazareth. At a time when there is so much of degrading dehumanization in the World, to minimize the humanity of Jesus is to diminish the resource supporting the struggle for human freedom, dignity and self respect.[153] Christology from below affirms man and his day today life. Thus, while developing the Christology the human element and its context should never be negated at any cost. Samartha suggest that Asian theologians may legitimately begin their Christological reflections from below. This determines the reality of the present day life and allows us to see the pluralist context in which we live.

The context should be noted that there are secular forces and ideologies which touch human at many points. There are political and economical forces that influence the ferment within religion;

152 John Sobrino SJ, *Christology at the Cross reads: A Latin American Approach* (London: SCm, 1978), 351.

153 S. J. Samartha, *One Christ Many Religion: Towards a Revised Christology* (Maryknoll: Orbis Books, 1991), 133.

it also should be noted that cultural and religious factors influence human being very much. In Asia, the problem is that it does not seem to have a theological meeting point between those who are actively engaged in struggles for justice and who are involved in dialogues of other faiths. The former thinks of latter as irrelevant and latter often regards former as one sided. I think this dichotomy should be erased and both the element above and below should be taken in consideration while developing Christology.

Chapter VI

# Understanding of God: Paul Tillich (Part I)

## Introduction

Paul Tillich (1886-1965) perhaps the best known protestant theologian of our time made theologizing an honored and respected activity at the chief seats of American learning.

Paul Tillich's Principle goal was to make Christianity understandable and persuasive to religiously skeptical people, modern in culture and secular in sensibility. He produced a philosophical or ontological theology in which every doctrine, symbol and concepts traced back to one of the structures of being itself, yet the Bible remains his primary source of revelation.[154] He desired to interpret the great symbols of Christianity in terms of modern existentialist Philosophy, so as to make the power of Christ's message available to the men today. It is believed that Friedrich Schelling and World wars

154 Edmund D. J. Fortman, *The Triune God: A Historical study of the Doctrine of the Trinity* (London: Hutchinson, 1972), 266 .

results had put a great impact on his ideology. This paper is basically concerned with Tillich's theology of God. At the very outset, this is a very hard reading but it will be tried to present Tillich's concept of Being and the Question of God in an easy language. Here we will see headings such as: Nature of being, The Structure of being, the logical arguments of God, general definition of God, and the Actuality of God.

## I. The Nature of Being

As we discuss this nature of being we need to understand the ontology. Ontology is the study of being, and it is with being, man's being, and it is being itself, God's being, to which Tillich relates every part of the system. As we see Tillich's philosophical categories and structures are rooted in German Idealism. Finite being, for example, means primarily man, logos-being. Man alone has realization of being and is potential participant in all being. Thus, ontology is an attempt to understand the question: What does it mean that something "is"? This is the most basic question which can be asked. This question implies some understanding of what "being" is. Thus, we have to begin thinking with some idea because it can't begin with 'nothing'.[155] So even if one asks why there is nothing, one attributes being even to nothing. Philosophy asks the question of being as being. This is its basic task and the answer it provides determines the analysis of all special forms of being. For Tillich this is "first Philosophy" and is therefore the basis of all Philosophy. Tillicch says ontology is possible because there are concepts which are less Universal than being but more Universal than any… concept designating a realm of being.[156] Such concepts are called "principles", "categories", and they tell something about the nature of being. Man is able to answer the ontological question himself because he experiences directly and immediately the structure of being and its elements. Tillich distinguishes four levels of such ontological concepts: 1. The basic ontological structure which is implicit condition of ontological question-which presupposes about the subject and the object. 2. The element which constitute

155 Paul Tillich, *Systematic Theology*, Vol. I, (London: SCM Press LTD., 1951), 163.

156 Ibid., 164.

the basic structure of being. 3. The characteristics of being found in the existence; and 4. The categories of being and knowing- structures of finite being and thinking.[157] Thus, this provides a definition of 'being' and gives basis and content to the ontological question.

## II. The Structure of Being

### A. Self and the World:

The first level of basic ontological structure is self and the world. Thus, being has a subject-object structure. Man experiences directly in himself the structure of being as a whole. Tillich says, 'A Self' "is not a thing that may or may not exist; it is an original phenomenon which logically precedes all question of existence."[158] By 'self' he means a centered structure which includes both the central point from which action and reactions occur and the environment, area, or world in terms of which the centre is defined. Man however is not completely bound to his environment but transcends it by knowing, and willing according to Universal ideas and norms. Man is fully developed and completely centered self. He 'possess' himself in the form of self-consciousness. He has an ego-self.[159] So, the self doesn't stand alone; man experiences himself as having a World to which he belongs. So man can't be considered as an isolated point, he is always related to his world directly or indirectly.

### B. The Elements of Being:

The second level of the ontological structure is that of ontological elements. This level consists of three pairs of elements in polarity with each other. The elements which constitute the self- world and subject-object structure of being are: individualization and participation, dynamics and form, and freedom and destiny. These elements appear as polarities and are always seen in there polar relation.

1. The first polarity is **individualization and participation**. Individualization is a quality of everything (self) that is and

157 Paul Tillich, op. cit., 164.

158 Ibid., 169.

159 Ibid., 169-170.

therefore it is an ontological element. But, the individual self as a rational being participates in the World with its structures, forms and laws.[160] The individual self is a part of the World. Tillich says, "Man ... is microcosmos"[161] man contains within himself the Universe because he participates in the Universe through his ability to grasp Universal structures, forms and laws. This participation makes all kind of knowledge possible, and the participation which the finite has in the infinite is the source of man's awareness of God.[162]

2. The second polarity is **dynamics and form**. "Being something means having a form."[163] It is impossible to conceive of anything without some structure. In this sense form should not be contrasted with content. The form which makes a thing what it is, is its content, its essential, its definite form of being. The form of a tree is what makes it a tree.[164] For Tillich dynamics is not "to be", it is something about to be, Dynamics is potentiality of being, which is non-being in contrast to things that have a form.[165] In man the polarity of dynamics and form appears as the polarity of vitality and intentionality. Man is able to create a World beyond the given World;... this is his vitality...'[166] Man vitality is directed and formed towards meaningful contents by his intentionality and because they are interdependent. This polarity does justice both to creativity and permanence.
3. The third polarity is **freedom and destiny**. This polarity is most important for Tillich's theology because on the basis of this understanding, he interprets the doctrines of

160 John P. Newport, *Makers of the Modern theological minds: Paul Tillich* (Texas: Word Books Publishers,1984), 104.

161 Tillich, op. cit., 176.

162 Newport, op. cit., 104.

163 Tillich, op. cit., 178.

164 Ibid.

165 Ibid., 179.

166 Ibid., 180.

Creation, fall and providence. Freedom in polarity with destiny is the structural element which makes existence possible because it transcends the essential necessity of being without destroying it.[167] Man is not a thing and freedom is experienced by man as deliberation. Destiny points to a situation in which man finds himself facing the World to which, at the same time he belongs.[168] So Tillich says, "My destiny is the basis of my freedom; my freedom participates in shaping my destiny."[169] Destiny is not the opposite of freedom; it rather sets its conditions and its limits. So, he who has freedom has destiny. Things have no destiny because they have no freedom.[170]

## C. Being and Finitude

Being and Non-being: The third level of ontological structure is being and finitude. Only man can ask the ontological question because he alone is able to look beyond the limits of his own being and every other being.[171] Man is able to take this stand point because he is free to transcend every given reality. Finitude according to Tillich, is being, limited by non-being. Everything which is finite is mixed with non-being. Non-being is that which makes it possible for man to step back from and look at being, his own being, and make this distinction. Non-being appears as 'not yet' of being and as 'no more' of being.[172] This effect which non-being has on man constitutes his finitude. But, at the same time man is more than finite. In order to experience his finitude, a man must look at himself from the point of view of a potential infinity.[173] The power of infinity self transcendence is an expression of man's belonging to that which is beyond non-being namely, to Being.

167 Tillich, op. cit., 182.

168 Ibid., 183.

169 Ibid., 185.

170 Ibid.

171 Ibid., 186.

172 Ibid., 189.

173 Tillich, op. cit., 190.

Categories are the forms in which mind grasps and shapes the reality. To speak of something reasonably is to speak of it by means of categorical forms, through ways of speaking, which are also forms of being.[174] So, categories are forms which determine content. They are ontological and therefore they are present in everything. When we see the categories and the question of finitude we find four major categories or forms of finitude. They are time, space, causality and substance. So one can't express a rational thought without using some categories.

## III. Logical Argument for God

Before coming to Tillich's theological statement of God as Being-itself, which is answer to the question of God seen in human finitude, it is important to see the way in which a philosophical analysis of existence give rise to the question of God.

1. Tillich rejects the traditional arguments of natural theology for the existence of God. For Tillich, the concept of existence is not applicable to God. God is beyond essence and existence because he is the creative ground for both. Therefore, to argue that God exists is to deny him.[175] So, as the creative ground, he can't participate in the tension and disruption of existence.[176] According to Tillich the existing idea of existence is drawn from modern existentialism and can't be applied to God because it signifies estrangement and non-being and implies that being has fallen away from essence.
2. Tillich further maintains that the traditional cosmological and teleological arguments for God are failures as arguments.[177] In these arguments, God is derived from the World and therefore he can't be that which infinitely transcends the World. So in human finitude the traditional

174 Ibid., 192.

175 Ibid., 205.

176 Newport, op. cit., 106.

177 Tillich, op. cit., 208.

argument is fine but they can't answer the question of God.

3. According to Tillich a subordinate use of cosmological argument can be made, to show how the unconditional element of which we are aware immediately aware can be recognized in nature and culture. The cosmological argument from contingent (conditional) being to a necessary being raises the question of God as Being-itself who is able to conquer non-being and give one courage in the situation of anxiety. These arguments serve primarily to help make clear man's need for God.

## IV. The General Definition of God

Following the method of correlation, Tillich presents the answer to the theological analysis of being. The answer is described as God as *Being-itself.* God is the answer to the question implied in man's finitude; he is the name which concerns man ultimately.[178] It means what ever concerns man ultimately becomes God for him. The phrase, "being ultimately concerned" points to a tension in human experience. The concrete things only become the possibility of concern. The *ultimate concern* must transcend every preliminary finite and concrete concern. It must transcend the whole realm of finitude in order to be the answer to the question implied in finitude.[179] This ambivalence between the concrete and the ultimate is seen in one of the characteristic of Divine called holiness. "Only that which is holy can give man ultimate concern, and only that which gives man ultimate concern has the quality of holiness.[180] The holy always appears concretely in holy objects; something or someone is holy. The holy loses it character of transcendence when identified with secular, but on the other hand holy needs to be expressed and can be expressed only through the secular, for it is through the finite that infinite can be expressed.[181] Tillich considers this conflict between

178 Ibid., 211.

179 Ibid.

180 Ibid., 215.

181 Tillich, op. cit., 218.

the concrete and the ultimate in the concept of God to be the key to the whole history of religion.

Polytheism is an expression of the religious demand for concreteness in Divine. Monotheism emphasizes ultimacy as a reaction against this concreteness. Mysticism transcends all concrete expressions of Divine and tends to become idealistic monism. Christianity provides the answer with Trinitarian monotheism which can balance the legitimate, the demands of ultimacy and concreteness.[182] This is an attempt to speak of the living God, the God in whom the ultimate and concrete are united.

## V. The Actuality of God

### 1. God as Being

The fundamental proposition of Paul Tillich's theological system is that "God is Being –itself".[183] He has being, he is being, but he is not a being. If God is a being, he is subject to the categories of finitude, especially to space and substance. Even if he called the "highest being" in the sense of the "most perfect", superlative become diminutives (tiny).[184] God is the Ground and power of being; he can't be placed in a category with other being, even if elevated above them. Tillich uses the analogy of being (*Analogia Antis*). Analogia antis means God is different but we can speak about common features & categories of god which we see in our life. For example, we can see our love is conditioned but when God loves then it is selfless love. In his book ultimate concern Tillich brings is personal insights about God. He shows how theology is discussion about God and everything revolves around question of being. In this expression, no body has special privilege to know about being but everybody has right to know. Tillich says Being-itself should guide and search the meaning. Thus, being is the foundation of the meaning.

So, God is power of being in everything and above everything, the infinite power of being. "As Being-itself God is beyond the

182 Ibid., 228.

183 Ibid., 235.

184 Ibid.

contrast of essential and existential being."[185] God is not threatened by non-being but includes it as that which he overcomes. God doesn't exist as being. He is the ground and power of being. He is transcendent in that he transcends every being and the totality of being. So, everything that has both origin and its power to be in him.

## 2. God as Knowable

The statement that God is Being-itself is a nonsymbolic statement. It doesn't point beyond itself. Everything else which is said about God is symbolic because it is drawn from some finite experiences which points beyond itself to Him. The question arises: How can man know God? How can he apply the finite knowledge to infinite? Tillich answers that finite reality can become the basis for symbolic assertions about God because every finite thing participates in Being-itself.[186] Thus, Tiliich can say that the symbols don't give knowledge of God but does explain the possibility of knowing and saying anything about God. A symbol differs from a sign in that it participates in that to which it points; the possibility of this participation has been explained in the statement that all being participate in Being-itself. A symbol has truth (if) it is adequate to the revelation it expresses. A symbol is true (if) it is the expression of a true revelation.[187] Tillich maintains that primary symbols for God derived from self or self subject-side of the structure of being such as individualization, dynamic process and freedom.

## 3. God as Living

Life is a process in which potential being becomes actual being. But, in God there is no distinction between potentiality and actuality. So, we must speak of God as living in symbolic terms. So, God lives in so far as he is the ground of life.[188] Thus, theology may describe the nature of Being-itself, the Divine life, in terms of structure of being

185 Tillich, op. cit., 236.

186 Ibid., 239.

187 Ibid., 240.

188 Tillich, op. cit., 242.

as it appears in human life. We know that the structure is composed of ontological elements such as individualization and participation, dynamics and forms, and freedom and destiny. God's life can be described symbolically in these terms. But, there is difference, in finite life there is tension and conflict but in Divine life there is rest because there is no threat of non-being to disrupt the unity. Tillich regards the symbol of "Personal God" as absolutely necessary for an existential person to person relationship with God. So, God is equally near and transcendent also.[189] The personal God doesn't mean that God is a person. It means that God is the ground of everything personal and that he carries within himself the ontological power of personality.[190] God if not a being then God is not having a personality. God is always a source of action but he is not in action. Ground of being allows people to do which demonstrates that he is not passive.

## 4. God as Spirit and as Trinity

If God is a living God, he has both Spirit and Trinity. Tillich defines "Spirit" as the unity of power and meaning.[191] In the realm of the spirit the ontological elements are united. The spirit is the fulfillment of life, for it expresses the reunion of the estranged elements in the finite being. So spirit is necessary and an embracing symbol for the life of God. The statement that God is Spirit means that life as the spirit is the inclusive symbol for the Divine life.[192] The symbol of the Spirit provides the philosophical presupposition for the Christian doctrine of the Trinity and one must begin from Christology. God's life is life as spirit, and the Trinitarian principles are moments within the process of the Divine life. Because God is Spirit, one may distinguish within the Divine life the principles of power, meaning and their unity. Power naturally refers to God's creativity, and meaning refers to structure of being or *logos*; it channels the creative power of God to rational structures. The idea of God as Spirit unites these two

189 Ibid., 245.

190 Ibid.

191 Ibid., 249.

192 Ibid., 250.

concepts, indicating the nature of the Divine life as power which takes on a meaningful structure.

## 5. God as Creator

God is creative because He is God. "The doctrine of Creation... answers the question implied in man's finitude generally."[193] It is not a story of an event; it describes the basic relation between God, Man and the World. God's creativity is identical with His life. He is Creator because He is God, and He is God because He is Creator. Tillich says that, "we must speak of originating Creation, sustaining Creation, and directing Creation."[194] This means that not only the preservation but provision is also under the Divine Creation. **God's originating creativity** means that the Christian doctrine of *Creation ex nihilo* means that there is nothing prior to or along side of God with which, or in terms of which He creates. There is no second power or material co-eternal with God out of which He creates. It is the ultimate protection of any kind of dualism.[195] **God's sustaining creativity** is also known as the doctrine of preservation. Creation is dependent on Creator because only in the power of Being-itself is the creature able to resist the non-being.[196] This is the basis of doctrine of preservation. Tillich says, "Preservation is continuous creativity, in that God out of eternity creates things and time together."[197]

**God's directing creativity**: Creation has no purpose beyond itself.[198] It should be not thought of as serving the purpose of God glory (as in Calvinism) or as providing an object for the Divine love (as in Lutheranism). Such concepts, says Tillich, imply a lack in God, which Creation is suppose to fill. [199] Rather, one should speak of the *telos* of Creation, which is to drive every creature towards its own fulfillment. Such directing creativity is called 'provision'. The

193 Tillich, op. cit., 252.

194 Ibid., 253.

195 Ibid.

196 Ibid., 261.

197 Ibid., 262.

198 Ibid., 263.

199 Tillich, op. cit., 264.

meaning of the word 'provision' is not for-seeing or fore-ordering where God is mere spectator or planner. Tillich says, "God is never a spectator; He always directs everything towards its fulfillment. Yet God's directing creativity always creates through the freedom of man…"[200] Providence works through the elements of being; it works through all the conditions of human life and includes man's individuality, his participation, his anxiety, his finitude, his freedom and his destiny. The answer to the question of man's being is found in God who is the ground of being.

## 6. God as Omnipotent

God is the power of being, resisting and conquering non-being. "In relation to the creature, the Divine power is expressed in the symbol of omnipotence. The almighty God is the first subject of Christian Credo."[201] If God was anything less, He would not be God and He would not be the object of man's ultimate concern. Tillich says, if God's omnipotence is thought of his ability ' to do whatever he wants' then it is denied because God would become a being alongside other beings, a being who faced, with various possibilities chooses one. Therefore, Tillich suggests that it is more adequate to define Divine omnipotence as the power of being which resists nonbeing in all its expression and which is manifest in the creative process in all its forms.[202] The ultimate power of being overcomes the anxiety of non-being and gives the courage to be.

## 7. God as Eternal

Eternity is omnipotence in respect to time. "Eternity is neither timelessness nor the endlessness of time. The meaning of *olim* in Hebrew and *aiones* in Greek doesn't indicate timelessness; rather it means the power of embracing all period of time."[203] God is essentially and actively related to time. "In God's life however, the moments of time are not separated from one another. Eternity is an

200 Ibid., 266.

201 Ibid., 272-273.

202 Ibid., 273.

203 Tillich, op. cit., 274.

eternal present which moves from past to future without ceasing to be present."[204] This means that the future is open and that which is new can happen in history. Therefore, eternity must be seen as an eternal present. Man's time is threatened by a past which is no more and a future which is not yet and his present is nothing more than the moving point between the two. Thus, he experiences a radical threat to his being in time. Faith in God as eternal in this sense can give man the courage to face his anxiety concerning the past time and the future time, since the separated moments of time are unite through God in eternity. Thus, faith in God as eternal is the basis for man's confidence that he may participate in eternal life.[205]

## 8. God as Omnipresent

God's omnipresence expresses His relation to space. Pantheism extends God into all the space, which subjects God to dissected spatiality; space becomes coexistent with God, rather than a part of His being. God also can't be relegated to a particular space, for He is everywhere, since His power and creativity act at every place. Tillich maintains that, "God's relation to space can only be seen in His participation in the spatial existence of His creatures.[206] Thus, God's omnipresence overcomes the anxiety of not having a space for one's self.... In the certainty of the omnipresent God we are always at home.[207] God's omnipresent is the answer to the question of man's being in space.

## 9. God as Omniscient

The symbol of omniscience expresses the spiritual character of Divine omnipotence and omnipresence. It is related to the subject object structure of reality and points to the Divine participation in and transcendence over this structure.[208] But, God is not separate from anything. This fact of Divine life overcomes the anxiety of the

204 Ibid., 275.

205 Ibid., 276.

206 Ibid., 277.

207 Ibid., 278.

208 Tillich, op.cit., 278.

dark and the hidden things in the life of man, for nothing is hidden to God.

## 10. God as Love

Love is an ontological concept not an emotional concept.[209] God is love. And since God is Being-itself, one must say that Being–itself is love.[210] Love is the unity of individualization and participation. Tillich distinguishes four types of love. Love as *libido* is the movement of the needy towards that which fulfills the need. Love as the *philia* is the movement of the equal towards union with the equal. Love as *eros* is the movement which is lower in power and meaning to which is higher.[211] The fourth type of love *agape* differs from these three and represents the desire, not for one's own, but for others fulfillment. It is independent of any contingent reaction of the loved one; it is unconditional. This characterizes God's love for man. Tillich says that, man's love for God should be described as *eros.* But, *agape* is the norm and standard for every type of love because it expresses the ontological basis for all love in Being-itself. One of the valuable insights in Tillich's conception of love is that it forms the basis for and understanding of Divine justice. This understanding of God's love and justice is also significant for Tillich concept of predestination.

The doctrine of God as love, is the final answer to the question implied in man's finitude. we can courageously affirm our creatureliness only if we know that He who is the power of Creation draws us towards Himself in love. This love is manifest only in the appearance of Jesus as the Christ.

## Reflections and Evaluation

At the very outset, when we see Tillich thought it really opens up our mind to think. We need to see Tillich from the background he came and grew, and faced the challenges of a broken World. As being a person who had seen both the World wars made him more realistic and profound. When I first read Tillich I was not very sure of his

---

209 Ibid., 279.

210 Ibid.

211 Ibid., 280.

thoughts but as I began to see Tillich from his own background and need of that time I really appreciate him for his bold theology. The very first thought which I challenge is the concept of **Ground of Being or Being itself**. Tillich views that God if only seen as blessing and healing doesn't give much weight-age, but God when we know as being we realize the things. It is more important for us to know Him as being than to just receive some material blessings. Tillich says God is always source of action and Ground of Being that allows people to do things. This shows that God is in work and He is not passive. Thus, Tillich says we have to be reconciled to being. In the present world, this concept can really boost the oppressed and poor who are very passive. As we look into the Dalit and tribal context we can very well say that the Ground of Being wants them to be liberated and be happy. The present scenario excludes people on the name of God and religious rites, but the understanding of Ground of Being will elevate people to think openly without any bias because the Ground of Being is not bound by any religion, caste or class. Thus,Tillich says God is active participant in all doing. The Ground of Being wants us to involve in the challenges of the day and be grounded in him. Being itself only can give meaning in life.

The term Ultimate Concern is not something about theological treatment of God, but expressing the state of ultimate concern. Ultimate concern doesn't mean our action but we are drawn to God to know Him. God is revealing himself to us and thus God is not unknowable. So being itself allows being to exist. For Tillich, God is Being-itself and this one statement which is not a symbol. The first God is beyond our symbol God. This Being itself even corresponds to Hindu Philosophy of Sarguna and Nirguna Brahman. But for Hindu Philosophy the gap between real (Nirguna) and Sarguna is too much. For Tillcih the concept about God is not unreal but real. This real God is man's concrete concern. He is the creating ground, and sustaining power.

Thus, God is the answer to man's quest, and underguards, it protects and supports His being and He is the power of being which overcomes the non-being. He is the ground of being and participates in being and gives courage to human being inspite of threat from non-being. As He is the God of love He becomes the basis of courage to be. Thus human can feel comfortable in Being itself and be uplifted. The fear is eradicated by the power of being. In the 21st century this concept can really revolutionize the thinking and give a basis for all human to face the challenges of today.

## Conclusion

For Paul Tillich, Christian theology must be apologetic theology because it must answer the questions implied in the human situation. The structure of being is experienced by man in a subject-object or self-world and contains the elements of individualization and participation, dynamics and forms, and freedom and destiny. God is the ground of being implies the assertion that He is the Creator of the, Universe. So, God Being-itself is the creative ground, the sustaining power and the guiding will for everything that is. This element makes him a living God, a God who can be mans' concrete concern. Tillich theology being the great Philosophy has also many controversies regarding his concept of God. Some philosopher even ask the question, is Tillich an Atheist? Inspite all the controversies Tillich's theology was admirable and will be also for the ages to come.

Chapter VII

# History and the Kingdom of God: Paul Tillich (Part II)

## Introduction

The Topic of history and the Kingdom of God constitute the conclusion of Tillich's systematic theology. Tillich correlates the concept of the Kingdom of God with his understanding of history. This is because, for him, the symbol "Kingdom of God" is answer to the question of the meaning of history. History is a dimension of life and is actualized only in the realm of spirit. "History" is the most embracing of all life dimensions and the "Kingdom of God" embraces and expresses the fulfillment of Salvation.[212] History and the Kingdom of God were the central concern for Tillich in the early theological career in the midst of chaos in Germany just after the world War I in the 1920s. Therefore, to understand Tillich's teaching of the Kingdom of God we have to understand the concept of

212 John P. Newport, *Makers of the Modern theological minds: Paul Tillich* (Texas: Word Books Publishers, 1984), 144.

history. So, Tillich basic affirmation is that finite reality is estranged, but never completely separated from the ground of being. Our effort is to see and discuss first about the history and then the Kingdom of God.

## A. The Nature and Structure of History

### 1. A Definition of History

The Greek word *historia*, primarily means inquiry, information and report. The interpretation of the events which constitutes history always takes place in the context of a "**historical consciousness**" or tradition. A tradition is a collection of events recollected in terms of their special significance for a special group. Tillich says, "There is no history without factual occurrences, and there is no history without the reception and interpretation of factual occurrences by historical consciousness."[213] Historical consciousness implies a priori understanding of the meaning of life and indeed is controlled by that understanding. A historical event has a subjective–objective structure, which makes it a peculiarly human phenomenon. For in the first place, historical events show intention and purpose. Thus, Tillich says, "Processes in which no purpose is intended are not historical."[214] Secondly, historical events are products of man's freedom, resulting from his intension and purpose and so no historical situation determines any other historical situation completely. Thirdly, because historical events are products of freedom, they produce human relationships and contexts that are "new." And fourthly, historical events, in producing the new value and meaning, produce events of unique and significance. To this Tillich calls, "that they represent essential human potentiality, they show these potentialities actualized in a unique way…"[215]

For Tillich, the direct bearers of history are **groups rather than individuals**. Individuals are only indirect bearer of history. Man

---

213 Paul Tillich, *Systematic Theology*, Vol. III (London: SCM Press LTD., 1951), 302.

214 Ibid., 303.

215 Ibid., 305, see also in Alexander J. Mckelway, *The Systematic Theology of Paul Tillich : A Review and Analysis* (London: Lutterworth Press, 1964), 225.

actualizes himself as person in the encounter with other person within a community.[216] If a group is history, it must have a certain quality. This history bearing group is not based primarily on force, but it is base on the feeling of belongingness of the individual members which is expressed in blood relations, language, and traditions is upon which the group is founded. Groups are the bearers of history because they have a "**vocational consciousness**" which is the aim towards which they strive and a destiny they try to fulfill.[217] Such vocational consciousness is different for each group in each era. For Rome it was the ideal law, for France it was the leadership of intellectual culture, for Russia the Marxist Philosophy. The group is the bearer of history in all realms, but basically and inclusively, it expresses history through politics because politics is the constitutive function of the group. Even the Bible expresses its view of history in terms of a political state – the Kingdom of God.

Tillich views that individual can't be considered the bearer of history apart from the group. Tillich says, "Biography is no history."[218] Individuals, if they represent the group, may bear and shape the history, but as mere individuals they have no historical significance. History is the history of groups.[219] Thus, history can be seen as the interpretation of facts or the series of facts arising from free and purposeful acts of man in which he creates the new in terms of value and meaning. This interpretation takes under the control of a particular group, or state.[220]

## 2. The Categorical Structure of History

In his discussion of "Being and Question of God" Tillich presents the ontological categories of time, space, causality and substance in their relation to finitude generally. In this Tillich applies them to the dimension of life under the inclusive dimension of history. **Time and**

216 Ibid., 305, see also in Alexander J. Mckelway, *The Systematic Theology of Paul Tillich: A Review and Analysis* (London: Lutterworth Press, 1964), 308.

217 Ibid., 310.

218 Ibid., 312.

219 Ibid.

220 Mckelway, op. cit., 226.

**Space**: Time and space belong together. Time and space, however are independent in a proportionate way. For example, in the inorganic realm space is predominant, and this means that category of time is not as crucial for the understanding of that realm. But, in the organic realm, for example, a tree exists, the spaces (root, leave and so on) and times of these various elements are united in the process of growth.[221] In the animal realm, through memory and self awareness, the animals can enlarge its empirical encounter with time and space. In the realm of human life, which Tillich calls dimension of spirit, both time and space are unlimited. But, there remains the reality limitation imposed upon the spirit by the concrete situation. The spirit has a time which can't be measured by physical time although it lies within the whole of physical time.[222] The spirit may transcend a given temporal and spatial environment, but it is always forced to return to the concreteness of some space - be it a house, a city or a country - at some time. History includes all dimension of life, the inorganic as well the human, but it terms of time and space it points beyond them.[223]

So, human history, to a large extent, is determined by the struggle between space and time. In the realm of history, time is as predominant over space as space is over time in the inorganic realm. Time in all dimensions shows an irreversible quality; it never goes backward; it always runs towards the new.[224] Since time is united with the dimension of spirit, historical time is creative and aims toward fulfillment which is not relative. Space should be discussed in connection with time for there can be no time without space.

**Causality and Substance**: Causality is the order of things according to which there is condition precedent for everything. The general character of substance is underlying identity, that is, identity with respect to the changing accidents.[225] Under the dimension of inorganic cause and effect are separated. In the dimension of organic and animal life, the categories of causality and by substance again

221 Tillich, op. cit., 316.

222 Ibid., 317-318.

223 Mckelway, op. cit., 227.

224 Tillich, op. cit., 319.

225 Ibid., 321.

show unity by participation. So, historical causality is the embracing form of causality because of the fact that in historical events all dimensions of life are actively participant.[226] Substance under the historical dimension can be called the 'historical situation'. A given culture can be such situation. So, like historical time, historical causality is future directed; it creates the new.

## 3. The Movement of History

History implies movement, movement towards the new. Thus, history involves change but the question arises whether these changes are the result of necessity or contingency. Tillich speaks of historical necessity as Trend for history is never without change.[227] As every historical situation contains trends, so it contains chances. Chances are occasion to change the determining power of a trend. The movement of history may be described in terms of action and reaction, growth, decay and dialectics.[228] Tillich says without them no meaningful description of the texture of the events would be possible. But, along with this Tillich even warns of the danger that they must be seen in flexible structures within which history moves rather than a fixed framework determining history. [229] In Tillich's view the dialectical structure of historical events demands special considerations because it is an important tool for the analysis and description of the dynamics of life as life. Tillich says history moves in a periodical rhythm which is a question of periods. Periods are subjective or objective, according to the valuation of importance in history bearing group. No periodization is meaningful if it is not based on events in time and space.[230] The period creating events can be sudden and slow, both.

History moves not only in terms of the ontological categories but also in terms of the **process of life.** These processes which are self-integration, self-creativity and self-transcendence are united in

226 Tillich, op. cit., 324.

227 Ibid., 327.

228 Ibid., 328.

229 Ibid.

230 Ibid., 330.

the historical dimension as a movement towards a single aim. The **Self-integration** under the historical dimension serves the drive towards Universal and total integration. The **Self-creativity** function of life drives historically towards a totally new. **Self-transcendence** function of life moves in history towards Universal and fulfillment of potentiality of being.[231] History stands under the ambiguity life, and history can ask the question but can't give the answer of the Kingdom of God. Tillich sees progress as a step beyond the given and in this sense the whole history is progressive. But, on the other it might even mean it is approaching its ultimate aim. In this sense, Tillich doesn't apply the word to the function of life in history. So, he says within the realm of cultural Creation there is no progress.

In the light of these considerations, Tillich says, "A particular religion could not maintain a claim to be based on final revelation. The only possible answer to the question of progress in religion would be the coexistence of different types without a Universal claim"[232] This view can be changed on the basis of conflict between the Divine and the demonic in every religion.

## 4. The Ambiguities of History

History while running ahead towards its ultimate aim, continuously actualizes limited aims, and in so doing, it both achieves and defeats its ultimate aim.[233] This is the basis of all ambiguities of history. The ambiguities of history may be distinguished in terms of the function of self-integration, self-creativity, and self-transcendence. Tillich says the historical ambiguity of man's self-integration is expressed in the formation of empire. Empires are built, grow and fall when they have reached their aim. Tillich even explains that Empires are not simple products of man's will power, but more especially express the vocational self-interpretation of historical groups (e.g., Roman law, Russian social justice, an American liberty).[234] Such aims are not bad in themselves, but they have caused unspeakable sufferings and the

231 Tillich, op. cit., 332.

232 Ibid., 337.

233 Ibid., 339.

234 Ibid., 340.

loss of life and meaning. In the historical dimension, the ambiguities of self-creativity are expressed in revolution and reaction. The basis of this ambiguity is the truth that, everything new in history keeps within itself elements of the old out of which it grows.

The problem of the relation between the generations is not that of authority but that of the old and new in the dynamics of history. In order to make a place for the new the young generation has to disregard the creative processes out of which the old has arisen.[235] The self–transcendence function of life becomes ambiguous when that which is finite is raised to infinite value and meaning. In the historical dimension, this happens when either the old or the new claims ultimacy for itself which is the definition of demonic.[236] The claim to ultimacy takes the form of the claim to have or to bring the ultimate towards which history runs. This happened not only in political realm but also in the religious sphere also. In Augustine interpretation of history, the last age begins with the foundation of Christian Church. So, the claim of historical ultimacy is often expressed in the final stage of history. For Tillich the place of individual in history is of significance. He says, "Individual receives his life as a person from the history bearing group to which he belongs. History has given to everyone the physical, social, and spiritual conditions of his existence."[237] Tillich says, these all ambiguities lead to the question, what is the significance of history for the meaning of existence universally?

## 5. Interpretations of History, and the Kingdom of God as the Meaning of History

Every legend, every chronicle, every report of past events, every scholarly historical work, contains interpreted history. History may be interpreted in a negative (non-historical) or positive (historical) way. Tillich sees the negative approach in the "tragic" example of Greek thought. History in this view does not run towards a goal,

235 Tillich, op. cit., 343.

236 Ibid., 344.

237 Ibid., 346.

but in a circle, back to its beginning.[238] The glory of life here and now turns into tragedy because live proves to be short and miserable. There is nothing beyond or above this sketch of time which itself is determined by fate. Another form of the negative interpretation of history is found in the mysticism of Eastern thought of Vedanta-Hinduism, Taoism and Buddhism. In these forms, historical existence has no meaning in itself.[239] They recognize the tragic quality of life, but show no way of dealing with it except through mystical transcendence of life and they reject the necessity of transforming historical existence

In the positive view of history, we find progressivism is genuinely historical interpretation of history because it recognizes the fact that history is going somewhere. Another positive historical interpretation to which Tillich calls is transcendent utopianism. It is implicit in the eschatological mood to the New Testament and the early Church. In this approach, Christ has appeared to save individuals within the Church from the bondage of sin and guilt and enable them to participate in the heavenly realm after death.[240] Tillich's main criticism to this view is that it is irrelevant. It is unable to see any relation between the justice of God's Kingdom and the justice of the World. It separates the Salvation of the individual from the Salvation of the World in general and the group in particular. In response to this Tillich says it is the vocational consciousness of a particular group which opens up the true meaning of history. Only full involvement in historical action can give the basis for interpretation of history. The ambiguities of life under the dimension of history are answered through the symbol of Kingdom of God.[241] Thus, the Kingdom of God is the final and valid meaning of history.

**The Kingdom of God as the meaning of History**: The Kingdom of God is the final meaning of history because it grants fulfillment to man in every area of life. The first element of Kingdom of God is **political**: this agrees with the political realm in history and means not only that there is realm where God rules but

---

238 Ibid., 350-351.

239 Tillich, op. cit., 351.

240 Ibid., 355.

241 Ibid., 350.

most importantly that he rules over history. The second element of Kingdom of God is **social** because it fulfills the utopian expectation of peace and justice. The third element of Kingdom of God is **personalistic** one. The Kingdom of God gives central meaning to the individual person.[242] The fourth element of the Kingdom of God is that it is **Universal.** It is not a Kingdom of men alone, but it involves all the dimension of life. The symbol Kingdom of God in order to be both positive and an adequate answer to the question of the meaning of history must be immanent and transcendent at the same time.[243] Thus, we find that Kingdom of God offers meaningful interpretation of history as both saved in the present and fulfilled in the future.

## B. The Kingdom of God

### 1. The Idea of History of Salvation

The Kingdom of God means Salvation for human history and therefore creates in history a special history of Salvation. The history of Salvation is identical with the history of revelation, because where there is revelation there is Salvation.[244] So, the Universal revelation shows the Universal Salvation. The aim of the Universal revelation is affirmed and recognized in special revelation of Jesus Christ. Universal revelation is irrespective of faith and all will be saved. Tillich says that history of Salvation is not identical with the history of religion, or with the history of the Churches, although the Churches represent the Kingdom of God. Saving power breaks into history, works through history, but its not created by history. Another question which is related to this is that, how is the history of Salvation manifest in the world history? The history of Salvation is a sequence of events in which saving power breaks into historical processes. The answer is base on the Christian symbolism and central Christian assertion that Jesus of Nazareth is the Christ, the final manifestation of the New Being in history.[245]

---

242 Tillich, op. cit., 358.

243 Ibid., 359.

244 Ibid., 362.

245 Ibid., 364.

## 2. The Central Manifestation of the Kingdom of God in History

Christianity claims to be based on its central manifestation and therefore, it considers the appearance of Jesus as the Christ, the centre of history. The term centre of history does not mean a midpoint between an indefinite past and indefinite future not it indicate a midpoint in the cultural process. The term centre expresses a moment in history for which everything before and after is both preparation and reception. As such it is both criterion and source of the saving power in history.[246] When we call Christ the centre of history we say that the manifestation of the Kingdom of God in history is not an incoherent series of manifestations. Tillich denies that there can be no progress beyond that which is the centre of history. He says the only progressive element in the preparatory history of revelation and Salvation is its movement from immaturity to maturity.[247] The maturity was seen in Old Testament, the time was fulfilled and manifestation was seen. The maturing process towards the central manifestation of Kingdom of God in history is therefore is not restricted to Pre-Christian epoch; it continues after the center's appearance and is going on here and now.

## 3. The Concept of *Kairos*

In theological term the *kairos* idea is related to the centre of history as God's action in Jesus as the Christ. The New Testament has called this moment the "fulfillment of time" and in Greek, Kairos. The original meaning of this word, the "right", or "proper time", must be contrasted with *chronos*, which simply means measured time. The Greek used *kairos* to indicate any good occasion for any action. In the New Testament it is used to indicate the occasion of the coming of the Christ. Jesus speaks of his own time of suffering and death, and both he and John, the Baptist speak of the time of the fulfillment of the Kingdom of God. Paul speaks of *kairos* when he speaks in World historical view of the moment of time in which God could send His Son.

---

246 Tillich, op. cit., 364.

247 Ibid., 365.

The experience of *kairos* has occurred again and again in the history of the Churches although the term was not used. Just as the Christ becomes the centre of history again and again whenever he is received, so *kairos* occurs again and again. "… the great *kairos,* the appearance of the center of history, is again and again re-experienced through relative kairoi in which the Kingdom of God manifests itself in a particular breakthrough."[248] *Kairoi* are rare and the great *kairos* is unique, but together they determine the dynamics of history in its self transcendence.[249] In times of *kairoi* the power of God may be revealed in terms of Creation, judgment, destruction and promise, which being interpreted in the light of "*great kairos*" of Jesus as Christ, reveal the ultimate aim and the victory of Kingdom of God in history.

## 4. The Kingdom and the Church

The Kingdom of God includes the Spiritual community, and embraces all realm of being under the perspective of their ultimate aim. The Churches represent the Kingdom of God in Universal sense. In function the Churches are paradoxical: they reveal and hide. The Churches may even represent the demonic Kingdom, which is a distortion of Divine Kingdom.[250] But, just as man having ambiguity of life, can't cease to be bearer of the Spirit, so the Churches, inspite of ambiguities of history, can't resign from representing the Kingdom of God. As the representatives of this Kingdom the churches share in movement of history towards its ultimate aim, when they are under the power of Spirit they fight against demonization and profanization in history.

So, the power of the New Being will enable them to fight against all the evil.[251] This power is manifested in the Church through the sacramental functions. The manifest Church is not the only agent that witnesses to the Kingdom. There is also the latent Church which exists before the coming of Jesus as the Christ, and which expresses in

248 Tillich, op. cit., 370.

249 Ibid., 371.

250 Ibid., 375.

251 Ibid., 376.

a preparatory way the power of the Kingdom of God. So, Churches always have some form of the spiritual community within them. So where there are Churches confessing their foundation in the Christ as the central manifestation of the Kingdom of God in history there the Church is.[252] Tillich makes distinction between World history and Church history. Church history gives meaning to the World history. Tillich was very unhappy since Church was supporting Hitler and was backing which was demonized. For general thought Church history and the World history goes together or runs parallel for the cause. In broader sense, Church history gives meaning to the things. While the Church history as the representative of the Kingdom is both a part of World history and also that which transcends it, World history is dependent on Church history.

Tillich is not talking in terms of causality but he is interested in preparation and reception. world history becomes preparation to receive Christ and it has received it. So, the meaning is important-it is Divine revelation or Divine presence. So World history and Church history is to capture Divine presence.

## 5. The Kingdom of God and the Ambiguities of History

Tillich also speaks of the Kingdom of God and the ambiguities of historical self-integration, self-creativity and self-transcendence. In relation to *historical self-integration*, he says that ambiguities are implied because of the drive towards centeredness leading to ambiguities of power. In contrast, the Kingdom of God exercises power eternally. Therefore, every victory of the Kingdom is the victory over these ambiguities of power.[253] In relation to the ambiguities of *historical self creativity* he speaks that it leads to the problem of social growth, leading to conflict between revolution and tradition. The Kingdom of God creates a unity between tradition and revolution and overcomes the unfairness of social growth and its distractive consequences.[254] The *historical ambiguities of the self-transcendence* are caused by tension between the Kingdom of God

252 Tillich, op. cit., 378.

253 Ibid., 385.

254 Ibid., 388.

realized and the expected Kingdom. The implication of this for Churches as representatives of the Kingdom of God in history is that it is their task to keep alive the tension between the consciousness of presence and the expectation of the coming.[255] Tillich also relates the Kingdom of God to the ambiguity of individual history. He says, each individual is thrown into historical existence, from which they can't escape. As one participates in the historical conditions, more sacrifice is demanded. This sacrifice when accepted is what Tillich calls victory of the Kingdom of God.[256]

## 6. The Kingdom of God and Eternal Life or the End of History

The word "end" can mean finish in terms of clock time. This means that life at some time on Earth and Earth itself will cease to have existence in time and space. But end also means "aim" which points towards a goal. The end or inner aim of history in this second sense is eternal life. There are people who say that no description of eternal life is possible because of its mysterious and transcendent character. But, Tillich rejects this view and says, "the fulfillment of history lies in the permanently present end of history, which is transcendent side of the Kingdom of God: The Eternal Life."[257] He believes that nothing which is created in history is lost, but it is liberated from the negative element with which it is estranged within existence. Eternal life includes the positive content of history, liberated from its negative distortions and fulfilled in its potentiality.[258]

So, the positive in existence is raised to eternal life and is thus freed to participate unambiguously in essential being. Tillich is very careful to tell that this essentialization of finite being does not simply mean a return to an original state of essentiality. But, Tillich holds that the products of history can add ontologically to essentiality. Thus, participation in eternal life depends on a creative synthesis of a being essential nature with what it has made of it its temporal

255 Tillich, op. cit., 391.

256 Ibid., 392.

257 Ibid., 396.

258 Ibid., 397.

existence.[259] The negative element is not missing, but the power of non-being is conquered, exposed and excluded from eternal life and the Kingdom of God. The Divine life is blessedness through fight and victory.[260] The symbol of New Earth and New Heaven indicates the universality of blessedness of the fulfilled Kingdom of God.

In eternity, the true being- essential being is raised into unity with being –itself. Tillich says that the absolute judgment or eternal damnation is not possible. He says, "Absolute judgments over finite beings or happenings are impossible, because they make the finite infinite."[261] Tillich believes that the evil in every life is rejected and that which is positive is saved and raised to eternal blessedness. For participation in eternal life there are two symbols: immortality and resurrection. Immortality can be accepted as soul is seen as spirit, which include the body, and that individual life doesn't simply continue, but is transformed and raised to transcendent unity beyond temporality.[262] Tillich believes that man's participation in eternal life beyond death is more adequately expressed by the symbolic phrase "Resurrection of body". The total life of man, both physical and spiritual is raised, but it is raised only as it is transformed. So the Kingdom of God includes all dimensions of being. The whole personality participates in eternal life.[263]

## Relevance and Evaluation

The concept of the **Kingdom of God** is not other worldly but is related to here and now. Tillich wants to see the Kingdom which is realistic and involves human's affair of now and here. It is not something to do with utopian World but it deals with present reality of human struggle and challenges of life and human existence. Tillich makes concept of Kingdom of God more appealing to the present context and addresses the situation of today. Thus, **Salvation** is not something beyond but relieve from the agony and turmoil of this

259 Tillich, op. cit., 401.

260 Ibid., 405.

261 Ibid., 407.

262 Ibid., 410.

263 Ibid., 412-413.

World. We need to work for the upliftment of the society. Tillich holds the view that specific revelation and Universal revelation should go together. Universal Salvation is based on the ground of being. It is preparing all being to receive New Being. Specific revelation might deceive people and thus Universal revelation is more accepted. Thus, everyone is to be saved and no one is to be lost. Wherever the New being is realized, Salvation is found. This thought gives a human existence firm stand and opens ways for more authentic living. **Resurrection** is Divine supernatural presence which is the power of New Being which will help us to change the society. As there are many oppressions and pains this thought indeed heal people and boost them to go ahead with positive attitude.

In today's context, Church can't claim ultimacy because every individual is to come to the power of New Being and be saved. Salvation is everywhere and Church can't become exclusive in this pluralistic set up. We can't just hold to the rigid ideologies and get us away. We need to think wider and think of present rather than always thinking of otherworldly. The Kingdom of God is not just for Christian but all are incorporated because Ground of Being holds all being. We need to make present better rather than just holding to future and living an unrealistic life. The Christian Church need to participate in the human struggle and liberate people from bondage of all kinds.

Tillcih is certainly right in saying that Christ is the 'great' *kairos*. But, his thought leaves the possibility that there are lesser *kairoi*. If in faith we are really *en Christos*, can we speak of any other *kairos*, but the one found in him? What actually does mean that from time to time we may receive other *kairos*? I think on these lines we need to think more and come to one conclusion that there is one *kairos* and that is Jesus Christ. Since, for Tillich Christ is just a symbol and he himself is not ultimate reality brings the notion of acceptance of all religion and calls for a dialogue process. Thus, for today's World, Tillich approach can be very well appreciated with certain carefulness.

## Conclusion

History for Tillich is not simply everything that has happened in the past, but rather it is the interpretation of purposeful acts of men in terms of the self-consciousness. History by its nature has the character of meaning and purpose. Historical time not only goes forward, but drives towards fulfillment. The World history and Church history are not to bring together but it is more to capture Divine presence. So, Church history and World history goes together and Church history gives meaning to things.

The Kingdom of God can be the answer to the ambiguities of history because it has appeared as the center of history in Jesus as the Christ. The Kingdom of God may appear through political system, a revolution, a Church or an individual and it heals the conflict in history. But, the ultimate and the final answer to history is not found in history, but at the end of history. This means that all beings is raised to the unity of ground and power of being. So, nothing created is lost and the most adequate symbol for the final answer to history is resurrection. Thus, Tillich uses the great proposition in correlating history and the Kingdom of God.

Chapter VIII

# Tillich's Appraisal of Buddhism in Interreligious Dialogue

## Introduction

Paul Tillich is known as the most creative theologian of the 20th century whose work is original and outstanding. "His thought reveals the influence of a re-awakened interest in world religions."[264] He loved Greek Philosophy and mythology and admired the vision of Parmenides and Heraclitus. His teacher Martin Kahler showed the dangers of narrowness, dogmatism and exclusiveness. Schelling taught him that religion can't be assigned to one particular human function but has to be regarded as the all embracing function of man's spiritual life. Troeltsch suggested him the value of interpretation of religious ideas, which seemed to Tillich to be in accord with conception of Christian universalism and freedom from ecclesiastical narrowness.

264 G. Richards, "Paul Tillich and Inter Religious Dialogue," *Bulletin of Rama Krishna Mission* Vol. 27 (1976), 225.

Tillich's approach to interreligious dialogue reflects his wider view of religion as the state of being grasped by an ultimate concern. The content of ultimate concern, which a man takes with unconditional seriousness, has the character and quality of the holy. The holy in turn consists of three elements which determine types of religion. The first element is the **sacramental element** which is the way the holy manifests itself through particular events, persons, and things. The second element is **mystical** which opposes any attempt to particularize the holy or objectify the ultimate. The third element is **prophetic** which opposes demonic forms of the holy, forms which deny the virtues of justice and love.[265] Tillich applied his type of interreligious dialogue to the relation between Christianity and Buddhism. Tillich suggests that the three elements of the holy are characteristic of all religions, and they form an excellent basis for mutual understanding and dialogue.

## The Concept of Religion

Religion is the state of being grasped by an ultimate concern, a concern which qualifies all other concerns as preliminary and itself contains the answer to the question of the meaning of our life.[266] The predominant religious name for the content of such concern is God-a God or Gods. In nontheistic religions Divine qualities are ascribed to a sacred object or an all pervading power or a highest principle as Brahma or the One. In secular quasi-religions the ultimate concern is directed towards objects like nation, science, particular form or stage of society, or a highest ideal of humanity, which are then considered Divine.[267] Tillich says that the main characteristics of the present encounter of the World religions is their encounter with the quasi-religions of our time. Tillich says Fascism and Communism are the most extreme examples of quasi religion today. In this two, the national and social concerns are elevate to unlimited ultimacy.

265 G. Richards, "Paul Tillich and Inter Religious Dialogue," *Bulletin of Rama Krishna Mission* Vol. 27 (1976), 226.

266 Paul Tillich, *Christianity and the Encounter of the world Religions* (New York: Columbia University Press, 1963), 4.

267 Ibid., 5.

## Christian Principle of Judging Non-Christian Religions

To start this topic, Tillich puts before some questions and expounds them. What has the Christianity, in the course of its history, thought about other religions in general and certain religions in particular? How did it meet them? What has been and what will be the attitude of Christianity to the powerful quasi-religions which are in their modern for? In this context, Tillich says Christians affirm the fundamental assertion that Jesus is the Christ and reject what denies this assertion. So, anything which contradicts with Christian principle is denied.

He says the problem is not the right of rejection but the nature of this rejection. Tillich says it can be *rejection of everything* for which the opposite group stands; it can be a *partial rejection* together with partial acceptance of assertions of opposite groups; or it can be *dialectical union of rejection* and acceptance in the relation of the two groups.[268] In the first case, the rejected religion is considered false, so that no communication between the two contradictory positions is possible. In the second case, some assertions of the one or the other side are considered false, others true. This is more tolerant than the attitude of total negation. The third way of rejecting other religions is a dialectical union of acceptance and rejection, with all the tensions, uncertainties, and changes which such dialectical implies. If we look into the history of Christianity as a whole, we can see the latter response in the attitude of Christina thinking.

Tillich says the indefiniteness of the attitude towards strange religions starts in the Old Testament. In the earlier prophets, the Pagan Gods were treated as powers inferior to the power of Jahweh, but they are regarded as the competing realities. In the long run, their loss of power led their loss of being; a God without ultimate power is a nothing.[269] Jahweh has superior power because he is the God of justice. On these backgrounds, Tillich builds his encounter with the Buddhism. Thus, he takes the form of dialogue taking in consideration the basic principles of Buddhism.

---

268 Paul Tillich, op. cit., 29.

269 Ibid., 31.

## The Basis of Dialogue

Tillich says in order to have meaningful dialogue with Buddhism it is necessary to determine the systematic place of both Christianity and Buddhism with the whole of man's religious existence. He says we need to know types of religion, general characteristics and their positions in relation to each other. Thus, he says in this context it will be impossible to call Christianity the absolute religion. He wishes to use the **dynamic typology** under which every dialogue between religions is accompanied by a silent dialogue within the representatives of each of the participating religions.[270] Tillich says Christianity and Buddhism grow out of a sacramental basis, out of experience of the holy as present here and now, in this thing, this person, and this event. This happens in two directions, the *mystical and ethical*, according to the two elements of the experience of the holy as being.

Buddhism and Christianity have encountered each other since early times say Tillich. Buddhism made its first noticeable impact on western thought in the Philosophy of Schopenhauer. The second influx of Indian, including Buddhist ideas occurred when Buddhist source were published by men like Rudolf Otto in book , titled '*The Idea of Holy*' which lead for dialogue between Christianity and Indian Religions. In relation to this Tillich asks question whether there is any impact of Christianity on Buddhism. He says in three ways Christianity could have influenced Buddhism: the direct missionary way, the indirect cultural way, and the personal dialogue way.[271]

## The Presuppositions of Dialogue

A dialogue between representatives of different religions has several presuppositions. It first presupposes that both partners *acknowledges the value of the other's religious conviction* (as based ultimately on a revelatory experience), so that they consider the dialogue worthwhile. Second, it presupposes that each of them is able *to represent his own religious basis with conviction*, so that the dialogue is serious confrontation. Third, it presupposes a *common ground* which makes

270 Paul Tillich, op. cit., 57.

271 Ibid., 60.

both dialogue and conflicts possible. Fourth, the *openness of both sides to criticism* directed against their own religious basis. Tillich says if these presuppositions are realized then the dialogue will be more fruitful.

## The Question of Existence in Christianity and Buddhism

Tillich says the question of the intrinsic aim of existence-in Greek, the *telos* of all existing things is the starting point for any interreligious dialogue and not the comparison and contrast of the concepts of God or man or history or Salvation. In the dialogue between Christianity and Buddhism two *telos* formulas can be understood: in Christianity the *telos* of everyone and everything united in the **Kingdom of God**; in Buddhism the telos of everything and everyone fulfilled in the **Nirvana**.[272] Both terms are symbols. The Kingdom of God is a social, political, and personalistic symbol. The symbolic material is taken from a ruler of a realm who establishes a reign of justice and peace. In contrast to it, Nirvana is an ontological symbol. Its material is taken from the experience of finitude, separation, blindness, suffering, and in answer to all this, the image of the blessed oneness of everything, beyond finitude and error, in the ultimate Ground of Being.

Tillich says in spite of this profound contrast a dialogue is possible between the two. Both are based on a negative valuation of existence: the **Kingdom of God** stands against the kingdoms of this World, namely the demonic power-structures which rule in history an personal life; **Nirvana** stands against the World of seeming reality as the true reality from which the individual things come and to which they are destine to return. But, from this common premise the difference arise. In Christianity, the World is seen as Creation and therefore as essentially good, proves the great assertion, "and behold, it was very good." In Buddhism, the fact that there is a World is the result of an ontological fall into finitude.[273] The **Ultimate** in Christianity is symbolized in personal categories, the Ultimate in Buddhism in transpersonal categories, for example, "absolute non-being." **Man** in Christianity is responsible for the fall and is

272 Paul Tillich, op. cit., 64.

273 Ibid., 65.

considered a sinner; man in Buddhism is a finite creature bound to the wheel of life with self-affirmation, blindness and suffering.

## Theological Concepts: Christianity and Buddhism

At this point, we ask the question whether the nature of the holy has not forced both sides to include, at least by implication, elements which are predominant on the other side. Tillich says if we look Christianity as a whole, we find large amount of mystical and sacramental elements, and ideas about God which approximate Buddhist concepts. The *esse ipsum*, being itself, of the classical Christian doctrine of God, is a transpersonal category enables to understand the meaning of absolute nothingness in Buddhist thought.[274] So, the idea of holy and the genuine experience of holy is not lacking in any religion. Tillich says this doesn't mean that a fusion of the Christian and Buddhist idea of God is possible. A living religion comes to life only if new revelatory experiences appear.

This leads us to ask the question whether Kingdom of God and Nirvana are mutually exclusive. Tillich says if in Paul, the Kingdom of God is identified with expectation of God being all in all (or for all), if it replace by eternal life, this has a strong affinity to the praise of Nirvana as the state of transtemporal blessedness.

But with this there are very clear differences also. Such as the symbols Kingdom of God and Nirvana, **participation and identity**. One participates, as an individual being, in the Kingdom of God. One is identical with everything that is in Nirvana.[275] This leads immediately to a different relation of man to nature. The attitudes towards nature in Christianity and Buddhism are not totally exclusive. Buddhist determined cultures are the significance of the principle of identity for the relation of man to man and to a society. Compassion is a state in which he who doesn't suffer his own conditions may suffer by his identification with another who suffers. There are great expressions of compassion in Buddhism but this is not agape.

The issue of **History** comes into picture in relation to dialogue. Under the predominant symbol of Kingdom of God, history is not

274 Paul Tillich, op. cit., 67.

275 Ibid., 68.

only the scene in which the destiny of individual is decided, but it is a movement in which the new is created and which runs ahead which symbolizes New Heaven and Earth. With regard to future this shows a revolutionary character which shows transformation of society. There is no analogy to this in Buddhism. Not transformation of reality but Salvation from reality is the basic attitude. No transformation of society as a whole, no aspiration for the radically new in history, can be seen here. Tillich after putting all the differences between Christianity and Buddhism asserts that inspite of all this also there is still space for the dialogue and there is no time where dialogue can't take place. These differences are not the end of dialogue but will give us the insights or the better interaction.

## Conclusion

Tillich brings greater similarity and shows differences between Christianity and Buddhism. He speaks that these differences are there but it will help to understand the religion more clearly in the latter stage. There is no time to which can be called as end of dialogue but there are always possibility of dialogue an appreciate other. He says to some extent Buddhism takes history seriously because they also ask the question of its spiritual foundations. Thus, in this context we should acknowledge the value of other's religious convictions, have a common ground and be opened to all the possibilities to have a feeling of acceptance.

Thus, stressing the need of the inter-religious dialogue, Tillich recognizes that it is no longer possible for a theologian to work effectively in isolation from spiritual insights of all religions. This recognizes the basic unity of all religions in virtue of the interdependence and interrelatedness of the type determining elements of sacramental, mystical and prophetical. Tillich recognizes that every religion has in its depth, a clue to the meaning of ultimate reality, and when liberated through dialogue, points to manifestations of the Religion of Concrete Spirit.

Chapter IX

# Hermeneutical View of Karl Barth & Rudolf Bultmann

## Introduction

Hermeneutics in general is theory of interpretation. At the very outset, Howard Marshal says, "Many of the Christian problems with regard to Scripture are matters of hermeneutics rather than of authority and inspiration."[276] God has spoken in Holy Scriptures but the problem arises how to understand it. So, the primary basic need of the hermeneutics is to ascertain what God has said in the Sacred Scripture and to find the meaning of it. The second great need for the hermeneutics is to bridge the gap between our minds and the minds of the Biblical writers. We will firstly try to define the term hermeneutics, then see the historical development of theological

276 I. Howard Marshall, "To find out what God is saying: reflections on the authorizing of Scripture", in *Disciplining Hermeneutics: Interpretation in Christian Perspective*, edited by Roger Lundin (Grand Rapids: William B. Eerdmann Pub. Comp., 1997), 49.

hermeneutics and then come to the hermeneutics of Karl Barth and Rudolf Bultmann.

## Defining Hermeneutics

The word hermeneutics is said to have had its origin in the name Hermes, the Greek God who served as messenger for the Gods, transmitting and interpreting their communications to their fortunate or often unfortunate recipients.[277] **Bernard Ramm** defines "Hermeneutics is the science and art of Biblical interpretation. It is a science because it is guided by the rules within a system; and it is an art because the application of the rules is by skill, and not by mechanical imitation."[278] To be good interpreter one must learn the rules of hermeneutics as well as the art of applying those rules. **Carl Braaten** defines hermeneutics as "the science of reflecting on how a word or an event in a past time and culture may be understood and become existentially meaningful in our present situation."[279] **Werner G. Jeanrond** defines "hermeneutics is concerned with examining the relationship between two realms, the realms of the text or a work of art on the one hand, and people who wish to understand it on the other."[280] Thus, hermeneutics can be defined as the theory of interpretation having different dimensions, implication and concerns.

Hermeneutics is not isolated from other fields of Biblical study. It is related to the study of canon, textual criticism, historical criticism, exegesis and Biblical and systematic theology. In Christian theology, hermeneutics deals with the interpretation of Biblical texts. The disclosure of God in the Biblical text, which is place uniquely, has to be interpreted because it can't be directly understood in

277 Henry A. Virkler, *Hermeneutics: Principles and Process of Biblical Interpretation* (Grand Rapids: Bakers Books, 1981), 15.

278 Bernard Ramm, *Protestant Biblical Interpretation: A Textbook of Hermeneutics* (Grand Rapids: Bakers Book house, 1970), 1.

279 Carl Braaten, *History and Hermeneutics* (Philadelphia: Fortress Press, 1966), 131, cited by Duncan S. Fergusan, *Biblical Hermeneutics: An Introduction* (Atlanta: John Knox Press, 1986), 5.

280 Werner G. Jeanrond, *Theological Hermeneutics: Development and Significance* (London: Macmillan Press Ltd., 1991), 1.

general human experience. So, Christian theology needs to engage in hermeneutical reflection because it is concerned with the interpretation of the biblical texts and other religious texts, such as creeds, liturgies, theological writings and spiritual expressions.[281] It is to investigate and to find how different interpretation has changed throughout the Christian problem in Christian theology and to examine and understand the meaning for the present.

Hermeneutical problem in Christian theology was not fully recognized and understood until the critical historical method was applied to the Bible as a whole. Friedrich Schleiermacher (1768-1834) contribution to hermeneutics opened a new era in the development of this discipline. This brings us unto the roots related to the primitive Christianity which in it *kerygma* announced of a person rather than interpretation of a text. So, in this sense the Word of God is not the Bible, but Jesus Christ. Therefore, the text itself hides a first level of interpretation because we are not the witness of those who have seen but we have listen to the witness. Hence, we can believe only by listening and by interpreting a text which is itself already an interpretation and our relation to Old and New Testament itself is a hermeneutical relation.[282]

## Survey of Theological Hermeneutics

In the history of the theological hermeneutics in Christianity, there have been various methods adopted in the interpretation of the Biblical Text. During the post apostolic period there were generally two distinct ways of interpreting texts, the Alexandrine and Antiochene. The Alexandrine method of interpretation had an allegorical tendency while the Antiochene favored the literal grammatical method.[283] Until the enlightened period, Werner G. Jeanrond sees Biblical hermeneutics moving within these poles. By the beginning of the 19th century and rise of historical critical method and the earlier methods and the criteria's were questioned and a critical approach to Bible was evident. It was against the orthodox

281 Werner G. Jeanrond, op. cit., 5.

282 Paul Ricoeur, *Essays on Biblical Interpretation*, ed. Lewis S. Mudge (London: SPCK, 1981), 54.

283 Werner G. Jeanrond, *Theological Hermeneutics*, op. cit., 42.

dogmatism and Biblicism which called for scientific, rational and critical method of Biblical interpretation. Hence, a truly critical theological hermeneutics was brought in by the new philosophical world view.

The philosophical hermeneutics took the way from Schleiermacher to Paul Ricoeur. Schleiermacher, "insisting that theological hermeneutics has to reflect upon and respect the principles of philosophical hermeneutics, freed theological hermeneutics from any ecclesiastical tutelage and open up a new era of hermeneutical thinking".[284] He insisted that any theological hermeneutics should be based on general principles of hermeneutics. However, the hermeneutical approach during this period were accused of skeptical view of historical Christianity and regarded the Bible as a fallible human record rather than Divine revelation basically seen by Karl Barth.

The period from Barth sees the Christianity from a totally different perspective. During this time, many flaws in the liberal theology were exposed and liberalism was seen as a failure. Post world War I there was failure of liberal view of human and civilization moving towards perfection. Karl Barth championed the new movement and radically opposed the pre-war liberal theology, and proclaimed that God of the Bible must not be confused with human ideas about God.[285] This gave a new emphasis on the Scripture.

## Karl Barth: (1886-1968)

Theological interpretation begins with Barth and Bultmann in the 20th century. The Swiss-German theologian Karl Barth held a negative view of protestant liberalism and rejected theologian's reception of Heidegger's philosophical hermeneutics. For Barth, any close co-operation between theology and Philosophy represented a severe danger to theology.[286]

---

284 Werner G. Jeanrond, op. cit., 118.

285 H. Harris, "German Liberation" in the *New Dictionary of Theology* (Illinois: IVP, 1994), 387.

286 Werner G. Jeanrond, op. cit., 121.

## Context of Biblical interpretation in 20th Century

Before embarking upon a discussion of theological hermeneutics in the 20th century we need to see the context of that time and try to understand the actual need for a different thought pattern. On the basis of this situation only both Barth and Bultmann rejected the Heidegger's philosophical hermeneutics and developed their own approach to theological hermeneutics. In the 18th and 19th century the historical-critical study of the Biblical texts seemed only respectable academic way of dealing the texts. The new science and developments led to a rationalist critique of the foundations of the Biblical world view. The question was more acute when it was made known that the Biblical texts could not only be trusted as scientifically adequate descriptions but even their status as reliable historical document witnessing to God's revelation in time and space began to be shaken.

The contradiction within the Gospel writers and so on raised the question, how one had to deal with the contradictions between the truths, history and reason. It was seen that since this historical treatment of the Biblical texts could not ground human faith in God, further theological moves in the Biblical interpretation took place. Thus, a new context of the theological thinking after the First world War merged. Thus, in this context the theological hermeneutics of Barth and Bultmann can be seen clearly.

## Barth's Theological Basis

The structure of Barth's theology is thoroughly Christo-centric. The beginning, center and the end of every doctrine is the event of Jesus Christ-death, resurrection, exaltation and eternal union with God, the Father. For him Jesus Christ is the singular and unique self-revelation of God, the Word of God in person. From this basic affirmation of faith Barth deduced the deity of Jesus Christ.[287] Barth affirms that true knowledge of God can't be received through reason, nature, and culture but only in the event of Jesus Christ. The eternal

---

287 Stanley J. Grenz & Roger E. Olson, *20th Century Theology: God and world in a Transitional Age* (Illinois: IVP, 1992), 72.

God is to be known in Jesus Christ and not elsewhere.[288] Thus, Jesus Christ is regarded as the sole mediator of the truth. For he alone is the very being of God in human nature and the very being of human nature in God. Barth begins his Church Dogmatics with the hermeneutical-theological question: What is the Word of God and who am I in relation to God's Word?

## Theological Hermeneutics according to Barth

Barth felt that historical critical method of interpretation was not sufficient and adequate to address the issue of his time. Werner G. Jeanrond identifies some of the issues to be addressed: First, the synthesis between human morality and Christian faith had proved to be false. Can Christian faith could say something new to this shattered world. Secondly, the need of new reflection upon its Biblical foundations after the old theological mode had discredited because of its affinity to German imperial politics.... Thirdly, if the Bible was to disclose any meaning to those people at all, a different kind of approach to Biblical text was necessary both on the side of preacher and on the theologian.[289]

Barth's commentary on Romans was a revolutionary book in interpretation. In it we see that the subject matter of Paul's language is radically translated and proclaimed anew in the language of our day.[290] Barth rejects Bultmann's hermeneutical approach to the Biblical texts. He considers Bultmann as victim of philosophical and other decisions which had led him to the illusion that any human method of interpreting the Bible could sufficiently adequate to grasp God's revelation.[291] For Barth, God must always remain the subject who interprets us. This is to say that for Barth, revelation is not outside of Scripture, but that revelation is in the Bible and therefore, Bible is the witness to the Word of God. Barth says,

---

288 Stanley J. Grenz & Roger E. Olson, *20th Century Theology: God and world in a Transitional Age* (Illinois: IVP, 1992), 70.

289 Werner G. Jeanrond, op. cit., 127.

290 James M. Robinson, "Hermeneutics since Barth" in *The New Hermeneutics*, ed. James M. Robinson and John B. Cobb, Jr. Vol. 2 (London: Harper and Row Publishers, 1964), 22.

291 Werner G. Jeanrond, op. cit., 129.

"There is no such thing as a special hermeneutics. But, we have to learn that hermeneutics which is done and generally valid by means of the Bible as the witness of revelation".[292] For him all interpretation should be guided by the subject matter of the text which brings out the theological message from its historical background. Thus, we see Barth tries to unify historical criticism and theological interpretation in order to understand Scriptures subject matter.

## Rudolf Bultmann (1884-1976)

Rudolf Bultmann is one of the important New Testament scholar theologians of 20th century. His family was shaken by the world wars (two brothers killed) and thus this had kept a great impact on his theological formulation. Bultmann's hermeneutical principle dwells on the existential Philosophy of Heidegger his colleague at the university of Marburg, who took adequate consideration about human beings and existence. Bultmann searched for an adequate description of the human situation in which Biblical texts are allowed to speak today and in which these texts confront individual human existence. He was of the opinion that the reader must recognize the conditions in order to become better aware of various obstacles which come while reading the text. Bultmann tried to analyze the process of human understanding first.[293]

## Theological Hermeneutics according to Bultmann

Bultmann didn't limit his hermeneutical focus to purely material, i.e. theological, aspects of Biblical interpretation. Rather, he recognized the importance of reflecting upon the nature of the connecting-point between God's self-revelation and our human understanding of Gods' activity among us.[294] Thus, he tried to clarify the conditions of human understanding and thus felt the need to enter into discussion on philosophical hermeneutics. Both, Bultmann and

292 Karl Barth, *Church Dogmatics*, Vol. 2 Part-II (Edinburgh: T & T Clark, 1963), 466.

293 Werner G. Jeanrond, op. cit., 130.

294 Ibid., 137.

Schleiermacher engaged in philosophical hermeneutics in order to improve theological hermeneutics.

Bultmann spoke of the the Bible needs to be approached with all philosophical vigor and tools of formal analysis but also with critical examine of the pre understanding of the subject matter. He was of the view that realization of the God's self revelation in our human history depends on some form of pre understanding. Such a pre understanding is provoked by our existential knowledge of God. In his article, "Is Exegesis without Presupposition Possible? (1957), Bultmann formulated five things concerning hermeneutics:

1. The exegesis of Biblical texts must be free from prejudice (willful dogmatic imposition on text)
2. It is never without presupposition, because as historical interpretation, it presupposes the method of historical-critical research.
3. A life relation between exegete and the Biblical text and a resulting pre understanding is presupposed.
4. This pre-understanding is not closed, but open for transformation.
5. The understanding of the text can never be taken to be definitive, thus the meaning of the Scriptures discloses itself a new in every future.[295]

## The Concept of Demythologizing

Bultmann presented this thought of demythologizing firstly in 1941 (in New Testament and Mythology) which caused a storm of enthusiasm and severe criticism. His opening concept was, "the cosmology of the New Testament is essentially mythical in character".[296] He says, the world is viewed as three storied structure which is mythical view of the world which the New Testament presupposes when it presents the event of redemption. So, theology must undertake the task of stripping the *kerygma* from its mythical framework of demythologizing it. Can Christian preaching expect

295 Werner G. Jeanrond, op. cit., 141.

296 Rudolf Bultmann, "New Testament and Mythology", in *Kerygma and Myth: A Theological Debate*, ed. Hans-Werner Bartsch (London: SPCK, 1972), 1.

a modern man to accept the mythical view of the world as true?[297] Bultmann applied demythologizing in textual interpretation because for him, God can't be reduced or objectified in human language that is understood. Therefore, the mythological language of the text has to be interpreted in the language of the contemporary people. Thus, for him interpretation moves like circle. Paul Ricoeur puts Bultmann's hermeneutics as, "to understand the text, it is necessary to believe in what the text announces to me; but what the text announces to me is given nowhere, but in the text".[298]

According to Bultmann the method of demythologizing of the Biblical texts leads to an existential intensification of God's call on the individual believer.

## Evaluation and Conclusion

There can be no doubt that Bultmann's interpretation theory call for a thorough critique today. Looking at the development of theological hermeneutics we ought to appreciate that Bultmann tried to take seriously both the Biblical texts and the modern scientific world-view, and thus was among the first theological person to respond constructively to the hermeneutical challenges which had emerged since the 16th century. He opened a conversation between theology and Philosophy which must continue as long as theology wishes to engage in its primary duty, namely the translation of the sense of the Bible into respective world-view of human listeners. Paul Ricoeur appreciates Bultmann for developing his hermeneutics beyond Schleiermacher and Dilthey towards hermeneutics of meaning instead of a hermeneutics of the author.

Thus, in the study of Barth and Bultmann we can conclude by giving some remarks:

We could find that Barth rejects the entire hermeneutics initiated by Schleiermacher out of fear that it could distort the self revelation of God's Word, whereas Bultmann critically and constructively developed Schleiermacher and Derthey's hermeneutical insights in order to enlighten theological interpreters about their need to reflect

297 Rudolf Bultmann, "New Testament and Mythology", in *Kerygma and Myth: A Theological Debate*, ed. Hans-Werner Bartsch (London: SPCK, 1972), 2-3.

298 Paul Ricoeur, op. cit., 59.

their conditions and aims. Barth and Bultmann both were critical of historicist interpretation of the Bible without neglecting the historical dimension of the Biblical interpretation. Thus, we can find that both of them affirmed the position of Biblical text having communicative authority. They are very important because they both have influenced hermeneutical expositions developed after them.

Chapter X

# Contextual Discussions: Black Theology by James H. Cone

## Introduction

James H. Cone was born in Fordyce, Arkansas, a small town about sixty miles southwest of Little Rock. When he was a year old his parents moved to Bearden, which is fourteen miles from Fordyce. In Bearden, there was a small community of around eight hundred whites and four hundreds blacks. At the age of ten he received the membership at Macedonia, and by sixteen he entered into the ministry. He was a student of Philosophy and theology and received his Ph.D on Barth's anthropology from Garrett Theological seminary & North - Western University in 1963. He has taught at Philander Smith College in little Rock, Arkansas and in Adrian, Michigan.[299] Later he had joined Union Theological Seminary, New York. In the context of Black experiences and agonies he first wrote, *Black Theology*

299 James H. Cone, *God of the Oppressed* (New York: The Seabury Press, 1975), 1-5.

*and Black Power* in 1969. His others works include: *A Black Theology of Liberation* (1970), *The Spirituals and the Blues: An Interpretation,* (1972*), God of the Oppressed* (1975), *For My People: Black Theology and Black Church* (1984) and *My Soul Looks Back* (1982), *Speaking the Truth: Ecumenism, Liberation and Black Theology* (1986).

## Historical Background & Development of Black Theology

From 16th & 17th century thousands of black African from West Africa (Ghana, Nigeria) and other places were taken as slaves to North America (Caribbean Ireland). The main reason for great deportation was to work in the plantation of banana and cotton. Since whites were not able to stand to the heat they wanted the black to work and made them slaves. Thus, black Americans are the descendent of the slaves who were brought to America. When African people came to USA they came along with their religion and religious ideas also, but the whites decided that they should also be Christians.

They were put in the Churches but were not treated equally whereas at the same time they were forced to come to the Church. As the time passed they began to follow Jesus Christ and understand the Gospel. They were part of the Church but not given the leadership or any ministerial work. But in later years as the discrimination broke the Black Church came up. We find examples of African Methodist Episcopal Church (A. M. E.). These churches came out from the white churches looking for their own identity and equality. In the 19th century the civil wars broke out which was basically against the slavery. Southern America didn't wanted to release the slaves and there was war with the Northern America in which eventually Northern America own and it didn't divide.

## Origin of Black Theology

James H. Cone says Black theology has three major contexts in which it had sprung. Since, Southern States had racial discrimination there was greater rift and problem within the community.

1. In 1950s and 1960s the civil right movement broke and thus this is the first context for the development of the Black theology. This civil right movement is largely

associated with Rev. Martin Luther King Junior. Thus, the Black theology came up in the context of black struggle for racial justice which was initiated in Black Churches, which was chiefly identified with human rights, or with Southern Christian leadership Conference & National Conference of Black Church.

2. The second context is the book of Joseph Washington, '*Black Religion*'. He said black religion is not identified with white Protestantism or any other expression of American Christianity. He said these are not churches but religious societies. This book produced a furious reaction from the black clergymen and they vehemently opposed the book. Cone says that Black theology was created in order to refute the Washington's book.
3. The third context was black power movement. It was a movement of radical black people to remove their discrimination by whatever means the black people deemed necessary. Cone says the method included selective buying, boycotting, marching and even violence. Malcolm X had a Black Nationalist Philosophy. Thus, this black power went against the Martin Luther King Junior no violence. Thus, black clergy published a statement on July 31st, 1966 in New York Times which is called black power statement. This statement supported the Black power movement. The term Black Theology was first used in 1960s but in 1969 James Cone used the term first in published form in order to develop a contextual theology.[300]

## God of the Oppressed

James Cone says, "Christian theology is a theology of liberation because it is a theology which arises from identification with the oppressed blacks of America, seeking to interpret the Gospel of Jesus in the light of black condition. It believes that the liberation

300 James H. Cone, *For My People: Black Theology and Black Church* (Maryknoll, New York: Orbis Books, 1984).

of the black community is God's liberation".[301] So, Black theology is Christian theology because it centers on Jesus Christ. The book, *God of the Oppressed* speaks of Cone's experience and tells about the sources of black experiences, social context of theology, speaks of Jesus Christ and his relevance and meaning of liberation.

## Chapter I: Introduction

James Cone says, "two important realities shaped my consciousness: the Black Church experience and socio-political significance of white people".[302] The Black Church introduced Cone to the essence of life as expressed in the rhythms and feelings of black people in Bearden. At Macedonia African Methodist Episcopal Church (A.M.E.) he encountered presence of Divine Spirit which gave him aspiration for freedom.[303] Cone sees God as the frequent visitor to the black community and source of encouragement in all situations assuring them of their well being. The Black Church taught him how to deal with the contradictions of life and provided a way to create a meaning in the society. Cone writes, "In a larger secular black community this view is called "art of survival" but in the Black Church it is called the "grace of God" because it is an unearned gift from Him who is giver of every good and perfect gift".[304]

This grace of God Cone speaks in the given **black experiences** where blacks were ill-treated such as: the white tried to infuse the idea that blacks were created to be white people's servant; doing the work of plowing their fields, cleaning their houses, mowing their lawns, and working in their sawmills; were called uppity niggers and even is showed displeasure were bitten up by cops and thrown into jails. The black's didn't had any name except their first name or just addressed as "a boy", and if passed over sixty were called aunty or uncle.[305] The blacks were even excluded socially and from Church services. In this

301 James H. Cone, *A Black Theology of Liberation* (Maryknoll, New York: Orbis Books, 1986), 4-5.

302 Cone, *God of the Oppressed*, 1.

303 Ibid.

304 Ibid., 2.

305 Ibid., 2-3.

context Black theology differs from Western theology because their experiences are different and it is different in perspective, content and style. Thus, Cone says, "What I write is urged out of my blood", and out of the blood of blacks in Bearden, who see what I see. Feel what I feel and love what I love.[306] He gives the example of song amazing grace which relates to the black people experience and how they are saved by the amazing grace.

James Cone says, "I am black theologian and I therefore must approach the subject of theology in the light of the Black Church and what that means in a society dominated by white people"[307]. Cone during his studies of Philosophy and theology understood the heartbeat of black life as reflected in the songs, and speeches of black people. But, the problem of Cone was how to relate black religious experience to the knowledge of classical theology. He was not happy with the response of the white people and thus, he turned to Scriptures for the answer and thus in 1969 he came up with the book, *Black Theology and Black Power* and thus, the new approach journey started. Cone insisted that the theology has to arise out of an oppressed community as they seek to understand their place in history of Salvation. So, black experience reflected in sermon, songs and story had to be pondered.

## Christian Theology & Theologian

Like other theologians, Cone also believed that Christian theology is language about God. But Cone says it is more than that, "It is a language about the liberating character of God's presence in Jesus Christ as he calls his people into being for freedom in the world."[308] The task of the theologian as a member of the people of God is to clarify what the Church believes and participates in the liberating work of God in the world. In doing this work, the theologian acts in the role of exegete, prophet, teacher, preacher and philosopher. As an **exegete** he needs to probe the depths of Scripture exegetically for the purpose of relating that message to human existence showing

---

306 Cone, *God of the Oppressed*, 3.

307 Ibid., 5.

308 Ibid., 8.

that it is God's Word to those who are oppressed and humiliated in the world. As **prophet** he must make clear that the Gospel of God stands in judgment upon the existing order of injustice. As **teacher**, the theologian is an instructor in the faith, clarifying its meaning and significance for human life. As **preacher**, the theologian is a proclaimer of the Word, the truth of Jesus Christ as the liberator of the poor and wretched of the land. As philosopher, the theologian is keen observer of the alternatives interpretations of the meanings of life. In all roles the theologian is committed to that form of existence arising from Jesus' life, death and resurrection.[309] For this the right question should be raised, for example: what has the Gospel to do with the oppressed of the land and their struggle for liberation? In this context the right source should be identified which is a difficult task. The sources include: Scripture, Tradition, History and Culture-Sermon, Prayer, Songs and Stories.

## Methods for doing Theology

James Cone while talking about the **methods of doing Black theology** says that it should be different from classical traditions. Ha say if Ludwing Feurerbach is correct in saying, 'thought is preceded by sufferings and if Marx is correct by saying, that 'it is not consciousness that determines life but life that determines consciousnesses' than we should see what is the connection of life with theology.[310] The life of black slave and white slaveholder was radically different. The life of slave was slave ship, and full of traumas whereas the life of white was of master and ruler. So when master and slave spoke of God, they would not possibly refer the same reality.

Hence, black religion and white religion are different in their life and experience. Thus, when a theologian speaks of black religion he should consider the environment and ethos of black slaves. The back slaves believed that as God had delivered the Israelites fro the bondage of Egypt so also they will be liberated from American slavery. Their expression was found in songs and freedom was affirmed. So freedom for them is eschatological a vision of new

309 Cone, *God of the Oppressed*, 8-9.

310 Ibid., 10.

heaven and Earth a freedom of future.[311] They use examples such as: Mary Magdalene and they called Jesus as, wheel in the middle of the wheel and, the Rose of Sharon and Lord of Life".[312] This is because Jesus gave meaning to blacks and was ever present help in trouble. James Cone respects the decision of Nicean council but says that source is inadequate to find meaning of black folk's Jesus. He says the question of *homoousia* is not a black question. Blacks do not ask whether Jesus is one with the Father or Divine or human. They ask whether Jesus is walking with them, whether they can call him up on the "telephone line of prayer" and tell him all about their troubles.[313] So, Cone says, "One's social and historical context decides not only the questions we address to God but also the mode or form on the answers given to the questions.

## Chapter II: Speaking the Truth

James Cone starts by asserting that we can't do theology unrelated to human existence. The black theology should emerge consciously from an investigation of socio-religious experience of black people, as that experience is reflected in black stories of God's dealings with black people in the struggle of freedom.[314] If we are rooted in this context than out theology will not be limited to Euro American definitions of theology.[315] A black perspective grants free thinking in relation to African cultural history and thus enables to listen to the urgent call to speak the truth. This truth is not an intellectual datum which is entrusted to academic guilds. Truth is that transcendent reality, disclosed in people's historical struggle for liberation, which enables them to know that their fight for freedom is not futile. The affirmation of truth means that the freedom hoped for will be realized. Cone says, "We do not struggle in despair but in hope, not from doubt but from faith, not out of hatred but out of love for

311 Cone, *God of the Oppressed*, 11.

312 Ibid., 12.

313 Ibid., 14.

314 Ibid., 16.

315 Ibid., 17.

ourselves and for humanity."[316] In order to understand this truth we need to see what are the sources and content of theology.

## The Black Experience as a Source of Theology

There is no truth for and about black people that does not emerge out of the context of their experience. Truth in this sense is black truth, a truth disclosed in the history and culture of black people. Cone vehemently says, there can be no Black theology which does not take the black experience as a source for its starting point. Black theology is a theology of and for black people, an examination of their stories, tales and sayings. So, Black theology must uncover the structures and forms of black experience. As we look in the **sermon, prayers, songs and feeling of the people** we understand their experience which is **Church related expressions.**

# **Sermons:** So while dealing with the sermon, one must listen to the proclamation of the as disclosed in black Word. The Word and the proclamation in the black Church is more than the conceptualization of the theological doctrine.[317] While preaching the preacher should not be bound to white, academic conceptualization of the Christian Gospel. The preaching of the Word must itself be the embodiment of freedom. Black sermon arises out of the totality of the people's existence- their pain and joy, trouble and ecstasy. Firstly the truth is proclaimed, and than affirmed by Amen and then the truth transcends the conceptual analysis and becomes liberating event experiencing the New Jerusalem.[318] The # **Prayers** of the black people are not as the same of the white people. Sometimes black people in their prayers were more direct in their rejection of white people's value system. Thus, prayers were of the affirmation of the black identity. In prayer sometimes God is addressed as "mighty good leader", "the dying-bed maker", and the "soul's emancipator" which points to God as the living and ever present who grants freedom for

316 Cone, *God of the Oppressed*, 17.

317 Ibid., 18.

318 Ibid., 19.

the humiliated and stands for justice.[319] In black prayer soul is laid bare before the Lord.

# **Songs**: a similar emphasis is founds in the songs-spiritual, Gospel and other melodious expressions. The function of the song is to sing the truth as it is lived by the people. Truth is found in shout, hum, and moan as these expressions move to people closer to the source of their being. In these churchly expressions among others, the Divine One informs and discloses himself in black reality and is best defined in terms of black people's response in body and spirit to that Divine source may it be: shouting, moan, clap, cry or even silence. [320]

## Black Expressions as Secular or Earthly

These kinds of expressions are secular to the extent that it is earthly and seldom uses God or Christianity as the chief symbols of its hopes and dreams. They are such as animal tales, tales of folk figures, slave seculars, blues and accounts of personal experiences.

#**Animal and folk figure tales**, the emphasis is often on the wit and cleverness of the weak in triumph over strong. The hero of animal tales is rabbit.[321] Humor is an import element in black survival and it is often related to the theme of freedom.

#In the story of **folk hero, High John the Conqueror**, the freedom theme is very clear. He was a "hopebringer" and serves as similar function as of Jesus thought not identical with Jesus Christ in spirituals. He symbolizes the slave desire of freedom showing that they are not alone in the world. Unlike Jesus who came from Nazareth and taught in Galilee, High John came from Africa and took flesh in America. The messianic secret of Jesus in Mark is also present in the tales of John.[322]

# In the **Slave seculars and blues** are revealed another black expression sin song but God is not the subject of these songs. It deals with the concreteness of life contradictions without reference to God.

---

319 Cone, *God of the Oppressed*, 21.

320 Ibid., 23.

321 Ibid.

322 Ibid., 25.

They don't deny God but they simply didn't use God as the symbol of victory over suffering and pain.[323] In the blues black people sing about the tragic side of life and use the artistic expressions of tragedy as a means of transcending it.

# **Narratives of slaves and ex-slaves** are the personal account of lack people's triumph and defeats. There are a religious and non-religious slave, who praise master and who doesn't praise.

# **Black literature** is another expressions of black experiences. The notable poets are Harlem Renaissance (1920-30) Claude Mckay and others black artists who recognized that art is never for it own sake but people sake. Black art is black people creating values based on their experience and affirming the willing to invent new definitions and lifestyle with their struggle to be free. In this context Claude Mckay said, "If we must die, O let us nobly die"[324]

So the whole black expression, Christian and non-Christian, preacher and poet, deals with theme of liberation and transcendence that happens in struggle. To speak the truth to black people is to relate the story of our mothers' and fathers' struggles to out present struggles and thereby create a human future for our children. To know the truth is to appropriate it, because it is Divine action entering into our lives and creating human action of liberation.

## Black Experience, Scripture, and Jesus Christ

**Scripture**: The question arises that what is the relation of black experience as source of Black theology to the Bible, which is traditionally identified as the source of Black theology. For black people the transcendence reality is non other than Jesus Christ, of whom Scriptures speaks. Through out black history the Scripture was used for a definition of God and Jesus that was consistent with the black struggle for liberation. People like Henry M. Turner affirmed that, "God is a Negro", Martin Luther King Junior viewed that political struggle was consistent with the Gospel of Jesus. The study does not mean that black theology can ignore the tradition and history of Western Christianity, but it only means that our study

323 Cone, *God of the Oppressed*, 26.

324 Ibid., 28.

of that tradition must be done in the light of the Word disclosed in Scripture as interpreted by black people. [325] Scripture is not limited to the interpretation of it as given in that particular tradition and thus it must be interpreted in black context. The early Church Fathers interpreted the Scripture in their given context and we can't blame them for not interpreting for our context.

**Jesus Christ Subject Matter:** Having talked about the two sources of black theology (Black experience and Scripture) it is important to distinguish both sources from their subject which is Jesus Christ. The sources of theology are materials that make possible a valid articulation of theology's subject. Jesus Christ is the subject of black theology because he is the content of hopes and dreams of black people.[326]

# He was chosen by the forefathers, was their truth and lifted their burden and eased their pain & gave them a vision of freedom beyond historical limitations

# He was the basis of their struggle and made them a people.

# Jesus Christ is the Truth and thus stands in judgment over all statement about Truth. Black experience is a source of Truth and not the Truth. But the other side is that there is no truth in Jesus Christ independent of the oppressed of the land- their history and culture and in America the oppressed are the people of color- black, yellow, red and brown.[327]

# Jesus Christ is not a proposition, not a theological concept which exists merely in our heads. He is an event of liberation, a happening in the lives of the oppressed people struggling political freedom. So to know him is to encounter him in history of the weak and the helpless.[328] So the interpretation should be done in the light of the consciousness of the oppressed in their struggle for liberation.

# Can black experience exists independent of Jesus Christ: if Jesus is meant of whitish interpretation than yes but if taken as image of invisible God, Creator of all than no.

---

325 Cone, *God of the Oppressed*, 31.

326 Ibid., 32.

327 Ibid., 33-34.

328 Ibid., 34.

# Jesus Christ is seen as the "bridge over troubled waters" where black experience is meaning of the incarnation.[329]

Towards the closing of the chapter, Cone speaks of the issue of heresy. He says, heresy refers to any activity or teaching that contradicts the liberating truth of Jesus Christ. It is an action which denies the Lordship of Christ. Heresy is the refusal to speak truth and thus this question of heresy should be reopened in our time, not for the purpose of witch-hunting but for the sake of the Church's life.[330] There are certain questions which should be asked for the sake of mission of the Church:

# Can the Church of Jesus Christ be racist and Christian at the same time?

# Can the Church of Jesus Christ be politically, socially, and economically identified with the structures of the oppression and also be a servant of Jesus Christ?

# Can the Church of Jesus Christ fail to make the liberation of the poor the center of its message and work, and still remain faithful to its Lord?

Thus, James Cone says, "Any view of the Gospel that fails to understand the Church as that community whose work and consciousness are defined by the community of the oppressed is not Christian and thus is heretical"[331]. The social context of the given community plays an important role in understanding the Gospel.

## Theological Concerns and Significance

As the whole black theology is based primarily on the black experience and thus, the significance of it should be to read the Scripture in the light of people's experience.

- God is portrayed as helper, guide, faithful and liberator. Jesus Christ is seen as the bridge over the troubled waters

329 Cone, *God of the Oppressed*, 35.

330 Ibid., 36.

331 Ibid., 37.

means that Jesus is present and thus this should be guiding factor for the Church today.

- God should be same to all thus Church should fight for the inequality and injustice for the people.
- The Church should identify with the poor and exploited class such as Dalits, Women and other marginalized groups.
- The reading of the Word should be done in given context and traditional barrier should be either broken or contextualized.
- The cultural values of the people should be appreciated and not negated and if possible be used for the proclamation for the truth.
- The subject of all theology should be Jesus Christ and this should not be tampered.
- Lastly but not least, the theology should be interrelated with ethics for the betterment of the Church.

Chapter XI

# Analysis of the Humanness of Jesus

## Introduction

Of the well known trio of South Indian theologians, Appasamy, Chenchiah and Chakkarai, the one whose personal experience of Hinduism was deepest and most prolonged was Chakkarai, who became Christian in his twenties as the result of much thought and deep study of the Christian faith. Vengal Chakkarai (1880-1958) was born in 1880 in a well established Madras family of the Chetty cast in Tamilnadu. His father was a follower of Vedanta, while his mother who greatly influenced him, was a devotee of the *Vaisnava bhakti* tradition.[332] Chakkarai received his early education in a Scottish Mission School and then went to Madras Christian College, where he was deeply influenced by William Miller. Vengal Chakkarai was by training a lawyer but later worked for sometime with the Danish Missionary Society in Madras. He was also involved in national struggle and also involved in the Non-Co-operation campaign. He

332 Robin Boyd, *An Introduction to Indian Christina Theology* (New Delhi: ISPCK, 1969), 165.

was one of the pioneers of the trades union movement in Madras and in 1941 he also became the Mayor of Madras.

As a thinker and a lay theologian, he was prominent member of what became known as the Rethinking Christianity Movement. Thus, along with Chenchiah he was one of the founders of the Madras group known as the *Christo Samaj,* which worked for the Indianisation of the Church. He wrote two books, *Jesus the Avatar (1927)* and *The Cross and the Indian Thought (1930)* and many articles. Chakkarai in his book *Jesus the Avatar*, was concerned about the need for the Indian Christian Theology to develop its won theology or theologies to express its understanding of Christ and Christian experience. He refused to accept that Christian faith and Indian thought are dramatically opposed to each other. He strongly believes that God had spoken in diverse manners and at different seasons through his prophets and *rishis* to men, revealing to mankind his holy will and mind. God has never left Himself without a witness at any time to interpret his mind to men. Thus, Indian mentality becomes a means of help, not only the conscious but also sub-conscious.[333] Jesus Christ, as Chakkarai experienced Him, transcended all cultures, Western or Indian.

In order to understand, the humanity and divinity of Jesus in the writings of Chakkarai we need to understand the term Avatar (Divine descent) properly which has great place in the Hindu believe. For Chakkarai, Christology is the starting point of theology. He is of the view that the real and valid knowledge of God must begin with personal experience of Christ. Religion can't begin with *nirguna* or *avyakta* (unmanifested) Brahman. The Christian *bhakta* must begin with the *vyakta Isvara,* God made manifest in Christ and thus Chakkarai says, "We see God with the face of Jesus…; God is unmanifested and Jesus is the manifested…"[334] It is only when the unmanifested becomes manifest, when *avyakta* becomes *vyakta,* when Brahman becomes *Isvara,* when God is revealed in the face of Christ, then men can know him as He is. And such knowledge of God is the result, not of *jnana marga* , but of the way of *bhakti,* of love

333 P. T. Thomas, ed., *Vengal Chakkarai*, Vol. 1 (Bangalore: CLS, 1981), 35-37.

334 V. Chakkarai, *Jesus The Avatar* (Madras: Christian Literature Society, 1926), 172-173.

for God become man in Christ. Chakkarai says, it is only through the experience of Christ that we can attain paravidya, the supreme knowledge of God.[335] With this brief sketch in this paper we will try to see Chakkarai's understanding of Jesus' humanity. Chakkarai in his book *Jesus the Avatar* while speaking of the humanity of Jesus talks of concepts such as incarnation, Gospel affirmation and consciousness of Jesus.

## Humanity of Jesus

Chakkarai starts the discussion by asking question, What is meant by humanity of Jesus? He says the idea of the official Church, supported by the consensus of the Christian consciousness, has ever been that Jesus Christ was the Word made flesh, and that his humanity is as essential as his divinity. Thus, Christ's humanity is not merely that he conforms to our idea of what a human is but that he raises it to the highest level. In other words, he is the true man, the ideal man, or the man in all men; and our manhood is justifiable only to the extent to which it approaches the humanhood of the master.[336] Jesus humanity is clearly evident from the fact that he felt, suffered and died. So his joy and sorrow, his sufferings in body and soul, his growth in physical stature and wisdom, and last of all, his death, all no doubt point to his humanity.[337]

Chakkarai says there are other factors to be taken into consideration in the definition of his humanity, which is as transcendent and mysterious as his divinity. Chakkarai finds the secret of Christ's unique humanness in his prayer life and in his sinlessness. In the Synoptic Gospels, we see Jesus retiring into the wilderness and spending the whole night in prayer. Some writers say that Jesus never prayed with his disciples; except for certain brief statements and short prayers we have nothing that takes us into the inner springs of his religious life. But, Chakkarai says, it can't be held that all night long he went on repeating learned and eloquent words, the meaning of which disciples could not understand. The account

335 V. Chakkarai, op. cit., 165.

336 Ibid., 30.

337 Ibid., 31.

of transfiguration is the one key in our opinion to the inner spiritual life of Jesus. It is a narrative which leads us into the invisible and profound World in which our Lord moved habitually.[338]

The prayer life of our Lord is characteristic of His ministry in a unique manner and in onesense constitutes the mystery of His consciousness. Prayer is the central sphere from which all the aspects of the religious life radiate. This prayer consciousness or yogic mind has been manifested in the highest degree by the *rishis* of India and by the prophets of other land. The difference is that the goal of the prayer life of these prophets and saints is clear and obvious, whereas the purpose of the prayer life of Jesus and method and content of it are all wrapped in impenetrable; we will not say darkness, but light. In Chakkarai views if ever any set of men held the key to the understanding of his life, it was his disciples and those who wrote the Gospels.[339] So it is from this mount alone that we can survey the heights and the depth of his being. Jesus is *Sat Purusha,* thought we are not *asat,* we are dominated by *maya,* because the true humanity in us has been obscured by some taint and its growth is retarded.[340] Chakkarai says at least, a recognition of the mystery would add to our conception of his humanity. In other words, our Lord brought God with him into the world or rather his life was hid in an ineffable manner and degree with that of God.[341]

## Christ in the Synoptic

Chakkarai bases his understanding of the life of Christ on the Synoptic Gospels. He is of the opinion that all the books of the Bible are inspired and thus historical criticism can't minimize either the personality of Jesus Christ or his place in Christianity. Everyone ought to admit that what our Lord did, said and thought has more value to us than the speculations of the most daring theologians of the Church. Chakkarai holds that we should keep two things in

338 V. Chakkarai, *Jesus The Avatar* (Madras: Christian Literature Society, 1926), 32-33.

339 V. Cahkkarai, *Jesus the Avatar*, 34.

340 V. Chakkarai, *Jesus The Avatar*, 74; cited by P. T. Thomas, ed., *Vengal Chakkarai*, Vol. 1, 16.

341 V. Chakkarai, op. cit., 36.

mind while studying the Synoptic Gospels. First, since the Gospels were written after the Epistles, so some of the ideas found in them should be interpreted in the light of the prevailing ideas of the Church. Second, Synoptic Gospels themselves are a revelation of the environment in which they were written. They reflect light on the history of the Church.[342] So, from Gospel we can get some conception of his life and not from the Epistles of St. Paul because there are very less reference about life of Jesus in Epistles.

Chakkarai says the neglect of the earthly ministry of Jesus is basically because of two reasons. In the first place, there was the view that before the World ends, the Lord would establish His Kingdom. Secondly, the earthly life of our Lord was past and people were looking to the ascended Christ in whom Church believed. It was the interpretation of Jesus as the non-earthly and heavenly being that caught the imagination of people (Gentiles). So, it was the super-human or super natural figure of Jesus that was the object of their adoration.[343] But to the Jewish Christians and few Gentile Christians like Luke the earthly events of the Master were of the chief attraction.

Chakkarai begins from the baptism of Jesus as St. Mark speaks of the baptism of John is where Jesus first appearance is seen. From Jordan, after the baptism, he passed on to desert where he was subjected to temptation, hunger and fast. This was followed by the Judean ministry according to the Forth Gospel. After this comes the Galilean ministry and the preaching of the Kingdom of God, the crowds, the Pharisees, and the Scribes, controversies, healing miracles, and break with the religious leaders. From this time onwards he avoids the crowds, desires secrecy and withdrew into the region beyond Jordan. This was followed by confession of Peter at Caesar Philippi there he taught his disciples about his goal, the death on the cross. After this he left for Jerusalem, he entered the temple and the cleansing of the temple take place. He ate last supper with his disciples and same night he was arrested, tried and next day he was crucified. Then came resurrection on the third day as a real rising

342 V. Chakkarai, op. cit., 18.

343 Ibid., 20-21.

of the physical body from the grave.[344] Chakkarai goes on to say that, "in the empty tomb of Jesus were born the paradox and the power of Christianity, the flame and fire of the faith. In all these incidents we behold Jesus and his affinities with us, mortal men are real. His hunger and thirst, his exhaustion and sleep, his love and joy, His tenderness and anger are all imprinted on our imagination".[345]

Answering to those who deny the divinity of Jesus by saying that there is no evidence for it in the Gospels, Chakkarai argues that if there were such claims in the Gospels, people would have suspected the genuineness of the record. Chakkarai maintained that the Gospels were written after the Epistles, one may be sure that the ideas about his divinity were prevalent among the circles of his disciples, and if anybody wanted to include those ideas in the Gospels it could have been done. Therefore, the absence of such claim is the strongest proof in the favor of the genuineness of the Synoptic Gospels record.[346] The methods of instruction used by Jesus were not dogmatic. He never told his disciples who he was in many words. "It is the foolish teacher who does this just as the painter of the dullest quality writes underneath this painting that it is a mountain scene, or twilight glory. The student must be led to draw the conclusion himself. It was step by step hat he led them to see the full blaze of his sovereign personality."[347]

## The Consciousness of Jesus

Chakkarai further takes us to understand the humanity of Jesus and says that it is in the prayer that one realizes oneself. The realization of our being, that is, in prayer when it is most real and powerful, we get glimpse of what we are. It is in prayer or *yoga* that the injunction know thyself is realized. So, Jesus in his prayer life came know himself, and that he carried with him the knowledge into his earthly ministry and into his daily dealings with men around him. According to Chakkarai the classical passage which explains the self

344 V. Chakkarai, op. cit., 24-25.

345 Ibid.

346 Ibid., 26.

347 Ibid., 28-29.

consciousness of Jesus is Mathew 11:26-7 *"All has been given over to me by my Father: and no one knows the Son except the Father- Nor does any one know the Father except the Son, and he to whom the Son chooses to reveal him"*. From this Chakkarai makes three inferences regarding the nature of Jesus' consciousness.

1. It is clear that the relationship between the Father and the Son is emphasized.
2. Here, our Lord is making the claim statement that he alone knows the Father and the Father alone knows the Son and that the Son alone can be organ of revelation of the Father and himself.
3. Our Lord does not say that thus revelation is to be mediated by his words or by his deeds; it is to be mediated by himself. The plain inference is that in his time the knowledge of God came to men through him, and today, too the knowledge of God must be mediated through his continued presence and operation, and not by the study of even the Synoptic Gospels.[348]

Jesus' humanity seems clear from the preferential usage of the title 'Son' to which he loved the little most is, Son of Man. Jesus never used the *tile,* Son of God, but it was given to him by the Father. It was the voice from heaven he got the confirmation of it. His Sonship was never learned from any human source. It was the real structure of his deepest consciousness; it was the native endowment of his soul.[349] Though his filial consciousness was the fundamental and basis of his religion, yet this manifested itself in several activities and was vindicated supremely by his vocation as the Messiah.

In this connection, Chakkarai points out two tendencies in historical criticism of the Synoptic traditions which are ethical and eschatological. The older view of Jesus, the ethical view, was that Jesus was par excellence a prophet of God who revealed to men (human) the character of God and also the way of God. And a consequence of this he was rejected and crucified. Eschatologically,

348 V. Chakkarai, op. cit., 40-41.

349 Ibid., 42.

Jesus is viewed as being faded away. Jesus believed that the Kingdom of God would be ushered in the future by a supernatural act and he himself would the centre of it. Along with this he even believed that the Kingdom of God has also come. Thus, Jesus is both religious and ethical teacher.[350]

Chakkarai speaks of the messianic consciousness of Jesus which is indicated by titles such as Son of God, Son of Man, The Christ, and the Messiah vividly. The messianic vocation was the only time-ordained method by which Jesus as the Son carried out his Father's will for the humanity. He came to recognize himself as the Messiah because he was the Son appointed to found the reign of God. Chakkarai speaks of three conceptions prevailed among the Jews about the messianic reign. Firstly, The Zealots wanted the Romans to be driven out by violence. Secondly, there was non-violent, non-co-operation party who relied on God to send the Messiah to rid Israel of oppression.[351] Thirdly, the people as a whole except the Herodians, Pharisees and Sadducees palpitated with excitement and became uncontrolled when the messianic hope became kindled. Jesus sympathized with national aspirations of his people but opposed the violent methods.

As the term Messiah had political associations and as he wanted to conceal his messianic consciousness and function, he used the title Son of Man which was found in the books of Ezekiel, Daniel and Enoch.[352] Though the term Son of Man was not a political term, it was blasphemous to use it. To make oneself the Son of Man was the greatest crime in the penal code of the Jews. Jesus claimed by this term to be the founder of the Kingdom of God or Heaven. According to Chakkarai, this Kingdom was not a mere moral and spiritual reform that led to what is called conversion. It was the emergence into the World of time and space of the eternal World of God. Thus, he claimed the power to forgive the sins. This term showed his suffering and death. His death constitutes the foundation of the Kingdom of God and he becomes the Lord of the human history and final

350 V. Chakkarai, op. cit., 45-47.

351 Ibid., 50.

352 V. Chakkarai, op. cit., 19.

judge after suffering and cross. [353] To Chakkarai the death of Jesus was the central factor in the life of Christ. It was the mystery of his suffering and death that attracted Chakkarai most before he became his humble bhakta.

## The Problem of Incarnation

Revelation is the supreme necessity of the religious mind. Chakkarai says God has spoken in diverse manners and at different seasons through His prophets and *rishis* to men, revealing the mankind His holy will and mind, here a little and there a little. Thus, we have India's religious past from the days of *Rig Veda* down to Kabir, Nanak, and K. C. Sen. They have been sent by God as witnesses of the Light.[354] It has been recognized that the religious genius of India must form the background of Indian Christianity as of the religious heritage of Israel. The *dharma-sastra* and *darshana* were continued until the times of refreshing came from God in the incarnation of Jesus Christ. In Islam, the prophetic word came in the form of Quran through angel, in Israel through Amos, Isaiah and so on. In other words, the word of the Lord or the Lord's mind came into contact with the personal mind of the prophet in accordance with the mysterious laws of higher psychical consciousness.

Those who denied the real possibility of incarnation take their stand on the basis of infinity of God. Between the infinity and finite there is a gulf and so only angel communicated the message. In this line even the Son of God was created.[355] Chakkarai speaks against this and says God Himself is said to have appeared to men, and spoken them directly. Later on, instead God speaking directly to the mind of the prophet, it is an angel that announces the Word of God. In the Saiva Siddhanta of the Tamil land and in Old Testament religion we find a belief in the theophanies. That Siva is said to assume a human form for a time and achieve some goals. These are merely appearance of humanity without reality. But incarnation posits a different and

353 V. Chakkarai, op. cit., 53.

354 Ibid., 1.

355 Ibid., 4.

more intimate union between God and man, like that between the body and the mind or the body and the soul.[356]

The primary needs of the religious nature of man and not the mere demands of philosophical readjustment, should be the light on our path, leading us to a right estimate of the personality of Jesus Christ. The question is that our religious experience is of such quality and quantity as to lead to the conclusion that our Lord is God. Secondly, after seeing the contents of religious experiences, we should find out the intellectual form in which our conclusion should be stated. Chakkarai says, "it can't be denied that Christological speculations in earlier times arose out of the necessity to give expression to the Church's experience of the living Christ."[357] The N.T and O.T in which the coming and work of Avatar of God are described are themselves books of religious experiences. While answering the question what is the quality and quantity of the Christian experience Chakkarai says, the idea of Christ's godhead formed the original impulse to the beginning of all Christian experience. He starts by saying that a man called Jesus really lived and died in Palestine sometimes during the first half of the 1st century. This personality produced certain results on men's lives and mind which amounted to a revolution in their thinking and acting.[358] He was the alpha and omega the beginning and the end of it. In many ways, this experience is expressed: he is the Redeemer and Savior of human from the present evil age (Galatians), the wisdom of God (Corinthians), the final judge (Thessalonians) and the dharma of God (Romans). In him, people hoped for the restoration of Israel.

To find Christ is to find the harmonizing principle that will reduce the chaos of the facts into a cosmos. He is the liberator, because he is the perfect love. He is the life of our life, the eye behind our eyes, the heart behind our hearts, the atman behind us. He is our embodies conscience; in his light we see light; he is the unspotted mirror and image of God. He the social reformer and the patriot who weeps for his country, the friend of the poor, and the deliverer from the hands of the oppressor. He is the mighty friends: he is all

356 V. Chakkarai, op. cit., 6.

357 Ibid., 9.

358 V. Chakkarai, op. cit., 11.

things to all human and a near friends yet a profound mystery.[359] Chakkarai at the end in this context says what answer we are to give to this problem of problems?

Chakkarai says the experience which is the most original and nearest to his earthly life is contained in the New Testament which is most reliable record existing today. It gives the details of his life, teaching, and of the experiences his bhaktaa had of him after his death. So it is the Gospel then that are insisted on as the only authoritative document of the Christian Church with respect to the nature of Christ's person.

## Conclusion

After looking into the discussion we can find that Chakkarai was keen on presenting Jesus' humanity as well as his divinity together. He didn't try to separate each other but shows how these both are interwoven and can't be explicitly separated. He presents God as taking the form of human nature (avatar) in every sense may it be his life, suffering or death. He is of the view that the real and valid knowledge of God must begin with personal experience of Christ. Religion can't begin with *nirguna* or *avyakta* (unmanifested) Brahman. The Christian *bhakta* must begin with the *vyakta Isvara*, God made manifest in Christ.

359 V. Chakkarai, op. cit., 12.

Chapter XII

# The Pioneer of Counter-Culture Movement: Jesus Sebastian Kappen

## Introduction

The centre of our thought and interest is to see Jesus' transforming power who was pioneer in the counter-culture movement. He transformed the lives of men and women in the tiny land of Palestine which had become a model for the present Church also. **Bruce Barton** presents Jesus as, "the man of action who makes his great appeal to our present World of practical affairs.[360] Jesus broke through the barriers, bringing together Jews and Samaritans, Man and Woman, rich and poor. God's revolutionary rule is not something affecting only people's mind or their relationship with God, but also their life in society and their relationship with each other. The revolution

360 Alden H. Clark, *The Social Dynamics of Jesus* (Madras: Christian Literature Society, 1930), 5-6.

of Jesus entails the establishment of revolutionary society.[361] So, to announce the coming of revolution was to stir up the people and stand against the oppressive elements of the society. Seeing Jesus as the pioneer for the counter culture **Ernst Kasemann** says that Jesus was a liberal. He said that Jesus meant freedom and he had challenged the norms of his day which were oppressive for people. Jesus was liberal because he broke through the piety and theology of his contemporaries, brought God's promise and love in place of Mosaic Law, grace in the place of good works and associated himself with the sinners, tax- collectors and with prostitutes.[362]

## Meaning of Culture

An individual is born in a particular society to learn the life ways of people. **Eugene A. Nida** defines culture as, "culture is an abstraction, it is a way of behaving, thinking, and reacting but we do not see culture. We see manifestations of culture in different objects and actions."[363] **E. B. Tylor**, the father of modern anthropology said, culture or civilization is that complex whole including knowledge, belief, art, morals, law, customs, and any other abilities and habits acquired by people as members of the society. **Kroeber** defined culture as, "the mass of learned and transmitted motor reactions, habits, techniques, ides and values- and the behavior they induce".[364] **H. Richard Niebuhr** define culture as, "culture is the social heritage people receive and transmit, which is human achievement portraying greater values".[365] Niebuhr speaks of Praxis such as Christ against culture, Christ of culture, Christ above culture, Christ and culture

361 David Wenham, *The Parables of Jesus: Pictures of Revolution* (London: Hodder & Stoughton, 1989), 24.

362 Ernst Kasemann, *Jesus Means Freedom: A Polemical Survey of the New Testament*, translated by Frank Clarke (London: SCM Press LTd, 1969), 40.

363 Eugene A. Nida, *Customs, Culture and Christianity* (London: The Tyndale Press, 1954), 29.

364 S. M. Michael, "What do we Mean by the term Culture?" in *Christ and Culture*, edited by Jacob Kavunkal and F. Hrangkhuma (Bombay: St. Paul's Press, 1994), 12.

365 H. Richard Niebuhr, *Christ and Culture* (New York: Harper & Brothers, 1951), 33-34.

in paradox and Christ the transformer of culture. The cultures are forever seeking to combine peace with prosperity, justice with order, freedom with welfare, truth with beauty, holiness with life and so on. Vinay Samuel regards culture as "the most urgent frontier of the Gospel."[366]

**Sebastian Kappen** says Culture can be defined as, "the organic whole of ideas, beliefs, values and goals which condition the thinking and acting of a community of people. Culture finds conceptual expressions in ethics, Philosophy and law; symbolic expressions in art, literature, myth and cult. It is also embodied in economic, social, political a cultural institutions and structures."[367] Culture is thus all pervasive reality and goes to form an integral element of any social system. But, the relation of culture and social institutions are not only identical but also of difference even to the point of contradiction. A contradiction arises when social institutions have developed along lines which render them incapable of bearing the values which they were meant to realize. This shows that culture is not static reality given once and for all, but something which is caught up in the overall process of historical change. Thus, because of unequal development of culture and social institutions and the class character of culture are the factors for the cultural crisis.[368] This means that those who control the means of production and control the levels of power project their class culture is universally valid and imposed on the common and poor people.

In proportion as the oppressed classes realize the prevailing culture is of their master and for their class interest leads for an upsurge of mass discontent. In order to get things right there arises a need for people (individual or group) who will challenge the upsurge. So, a prophet or a pioneer appears on the scene as the focus of concentration of the crisis of consciousness affecting the masses as a whole. He identifies himself with their longing for a new social order, in which they will live their own thoughts, values, norms and hope. Hence, this prophet or pioneer represents both the masses and

---

366 Chris Sugden, *Gospel, Culture and Transformation* (Oxford: Regnum Books International, 1997), 62.

367 Sebastian Kappen , *Jesus and Culture* (Delhi: ISPCK, 2002), 3-4.

368 Ibid.

the Divine. In this particular situation, Jesus appears on the scene and helps, people and critiques the externalities of the culture and becomes the pioneer of the counter-cultural movement.

Thus, in this context we need to ask the question how Jesus is pioneer of the counter–culture movement? The main question is raised in concern for freedom from inherited culture bondages and freedom for fashioning a new, humane and humanizing culture. To understand Jesus we need to have knowledge of Jesus' cultural context and of the new vision and values he stood for. Thus, we will try to define culture and in brief see the historical set up of Jesus' time.

## Historical Background

In the time of Jesus, the masses of the people of Palestine were under the twofold cultural dominations. From the third century B.C a process of cultural symbiosis had been at work between Judaism and Hellenism. After the death of Alexander the Great in 323 B.C Palestine fell to Ptolemy's whose military occupation lasted till about 200 B.C. Pompey conquered the country in 63 B.C. The **Romans** allowed Herod to rule and have his way (41-4) B.C. After 6 A.D. Judea came under Roman rule directly, after the destruction of Jerusalem (Temple) in 70 A.D. The Roman rule came under Titus. The Romans humiliated people by subjugation and military tyranny. They oppressed the people by collecting various taxes like: personal tax, land tax, an annual tax to maintain the Roman army, and various indirect taxes and duties.[369] They misused people's wealth by living luxurious life and building projects. The Romans ruled through Jewish authorities: the chief priests, the scribes and the elders who formed the **Sanhedrin**. These people enjoyed the political and theological powers. It was the supreme political, criminal and religious tribunal as well as the great seat of state government or state power.[370] The central symbol of state and of the nation was Temple; the hub of their economic, political, cultural and religious life which became the centre for making money. The treasury of the temple

369 Samuel Rayan, "Early Christianity as Counter-Culture" in *Religion, Ideology and Counter Culture*, edited by Philip Mathew & Ajit Muricken (Bangalore: Horizon Books, 1987), 116.

370 Ibid.

was controlled by the priestly aristocracy for whom it was a source of income. The rich indulged in extravagances like, houses, clothing, luxury goods, servants and temple offerings.

**Galilee** was ruled by Herod Antipas in time of Jesus. But, the taxes were collected for which he used force. Peasants were subjected to religious taxes for the benefit of the Galilean priest and of the temple. In Galilee, the real power was in the hands of Pharisees who loved the best seat in the synagogue and salutation in the markets (Luke 11:43). They had power in both places: synagogue and market, Church and State. They were concerned with purity and pollution which made them the purer class. Contact with impure things made impure and the common people fell in the category of impure. They were almost excluded from temple, worship and society of the so called holy people. Pollution due to certain profession like herding, tax collecting and due to birth and race, entailed loss of civil and political rights. Thus, Pharisees considered other than them everyone in Galilee unclean. There existed a close connection between social stratification and ritual religion with pollution – consciousness.[371] Thus, there were rich poor and the destitute who formed the society of that time and it was in this context Jesus came to reform and announce the Kingdom of God and be a pioneer for the liberation movement of the people. The announcement on the one hand was a threat and a challenge to the kings and lords and to the wealthy aristocracy; and on the other hand a dawn of hope for the poor and the destitute.

## Jesus the Pioneer of Counter-Culture Movement

**Sebastian Kappen** says, "the time was thus rip for a prophet to arise who would help the poor and the disinherited to shake off their cultural shackles and march forward for new frontiers and a prophet did emerge: he was Jesus of Nazareth".[372] Jesus worked in situations of tension and clash of interests. He took positions and provoked the conflict. It determined opposition to greed; he stood

371 Joachim Jeremias, *Jerusalem in the Time of Jesus: An Investigation into Economic and Social Conditions during the New Testament Period* (London: SCM, 1969), 3-4.

372 Kappen, op. cit., 10.

for different kind of society in which humaneness should prevail. He presented an alternative; not in theory but in practice of the Kingdom he proclaimed the practice of freedom, justice and equality. At the economic level, he introduced the logic of giving, sharing and community of goods in opposition to the prevalent ideology of exclusive accumulation. Against the debt and poverty he brought the concept of abundance.[373] Jesus defined authority in terms of service to the masses. Jesus practice consisted in rejection of the dominant code of society, of the oppression practice of empire and temple. The resurrection is counter culture. It is the culture of life in full in the body against powers, secular and religious, which kill body in the name of spiritual abstractions. It is the living body breaking through the restrictions, laws and tombs in which it is forcibly held.[374]

With the coming of God's reign the new era begun which brought the substantial alternation of their situation. The Kingdom is not something abstract but it is a force which changes history in favor of the poor, which has a strong egalitarian structure. It encounters the class structure and class ideology of the empire and temple-state. Thus, freedom is the central theme of the Kingdom which removed religious laws and social conventions which was a yoke of suffocation. Jesus invited people/masses who were burdened and heavy hearted to walk his way which was free of oppressive loads.[375] For Jesus, the reign of God constituted the Value of all values, that Universal Value in the light of which the value of everything was measured. Under this new scenario, the last became first, and the first last. In the new social praxis the things, persons, events, customs and actions were evaluated. He became the pioneer for the counter-culture where he challenged the existing social and religious order and brought polarity between rich versus poor, great versus least, man versus woman, parent versus children, Jews versus Gentiles, wise versus simple and pure versus impure.[376]

---

373 Samuel Rayan, op. cit., 120.

374 Ibid., 123.

375 Ibid., 125.

376 Sebastian Kappen, op. cit., 13.

## 1. Rich versus Poor

Economic exploitation and its concomitants, poverty and inequality, have exited in one form or another in Jesus' time of Palestine. There was a wide gulf existed between the rich and poor. Under the rich there were Royal aristocracy of Herod, Sadducees, landlords, big traders and merchants. There were also middle class made up of retail traders, craftsmen etc. The bulk of the population belonged to the poorer classes such as *peasantry class* who depended upon landlords and were victim of multiple exploitations. The peasants were wage laborers.[377] According to Jesus, a fulfillment of the law which could correspond to eternal life consists in giving all one's wealth to the poor. The egalitarian origin of Israel and the dream of classless fraternity was cherished by the prophets (Is. 2:11-16; 11:4-9, 40:3-5), the law itself is seen basically as a counter-culture for the development of a new social order. Thus, in order to implement it one has to go against the existing notion and so Jesus had to do that.

Thus, the dominant theology attached supreme value to wealth, projecting it as a concrete sign of Divine favor. Poverty was held to be punishment for sin. This idea suited very well to rich who would have the comfortable feeling that they were close to God and they were not exploiting the poor. But, Jesus went against this idea and said the Kingdom belongs to the poor and blessing are for the poor and the exploited one (Luke 6: 20, 24). Jesus opted for poor because they were exploited and they were open for the Kingdom of God in opposition to rich who were self satisfied and closed for any change. In the affirmation of the poor, Jesus broke the cultural barriers which Pharisees had constructed of purity and pollution, law and order and submission to the authority of tradition. Jesus casual treatment of Sabbath therefore implied liberation of the people in the sacred sphere as well as in the secular.[378] Thus, Jesus associated with poor, outcaste mass of the time.

377 Sebastian Kappen, *Jesus and Freedom* (Maryknoll, New York: Orbis Books, 1977), 82.

378 Samuel Rayan, op. cit., 128.

## 2. The Great versus the Least

This polarity refers to the social distribution of power, and shows the relation between the ruler and the ruled. The concept here dealt is master slave relationship were later suffered and was without any identity. Few people controlled the life of all and this was not accepted by Jesus. He believed and preached about the total freedom open to all human beings. Jesus statement, "whoever would be great among you must be your servant, and whoever would be first among you must be the slave of all" should not be interpreted as mere advice but a call to radically renounce all exercise of power.[379] Whosoever wants to be great he should be able to put himself in the shoes of the least. Unless there is attitude of lowness no one can be great really. In social order in which all are slave to one another and none is master over anyone. So, Jesus not only rejects the division of society into the great and least but also speaks of the truth by which the worth of person is determined. Not command over but service to other is the true measure of greatness. He favors the least and powerless because they were open to the new humanity in which there will be neither ruler or ruled ones. In this way, Jesus brings a counter-culture idea by interpreting the meaning of greatness.

## 3. Man versus Woman

Woman was seen as chattel or possession in Jewish society and was openly despised and even was not allowed to move out without a veil. **Mary Daly** speaks of the regular prayer of the Jewish who prayed, "That he was not made woman, dog or bore (gentile) portrays the status of woman.[380] In Jewish community a woman had no claim on inheritance except when there was no male heir (Num.27). Women had no part in public life: seclusion was recommended an often enforced and even they were not allowed to speak in public. So, in the case of patriarchal societies, Judaism set a high value on man and relegated women to an inferior position. The woman was considered a source of moral danger and was assigned an inferior place in

379 Sebastian Kappen, *Jesus and Culture*, op. cit., 14.

380 Mary Daly, *Beyond God the Father: Towards Philosophy of Women's Liberation* (London: Women's Press, 1986), 132.

temple. **Myrtle Langley** points out that Jesus' acts were of revolution which had invited stern criticism from the Jewish clergy. He allowed Samaritan woman to give him water to drink and converse with her was itself a revolution.[381] Thus, under this background Jesus attitude towards women was for sure a counter-culture movement which had raised anger of the leaders of that time. Jesus didn't had any problem with women and he allowed women to touch him, accompany him, serve him and listen to his teaching (Jn. 4:27, Lk. 10:38-42, 8:1-3).

## 4. Pure versus Impure

The polarity of pure and impure is central to all religions and because it is here that the counter-cultural stance of Jesus comes into the boldest relief. The distinction between the pure and the impure has been from the primitive time but had become a menace in the Jewish culture. The pure is whatever contributes to life and impure whatever is detrimental to it. The pure was identified with the Divine and impure associated with demonic. Thus, all the mythical conceptions were overlaid with religious meanings. In this connection the hierarchy was developed under which the head assumed to be God, the supreme pure and sacred.[382] Among the Jews, this conception found its expression in the belief that the temple, especially the Holy of Holies, was the centre of the sacred Universe. Hence, the society was also based on the same gradation of purity. Priests formed the base and they were to mediate life Divine and to deal with sacred things. Lower came the lay people who were classified in terms of descending degrees of purity in respect to origin, profession, and like wise.

This gave power to priestly class to exercise domination over entire population. At the time of Jesus, Pharisees and Scribes were zealous in observation of the Laws of purity, while the general mass didn't care much about it. Jesus' attitude to the law of pollution is best seen in the controversies of Pharisees and Scribes regarding the washing of hands before meal (Mk.7:1-23). Jesus defended his disciples and asked them to honor God through heart not just by

381 Myrtle Langley, *Equal Women: A Christian Feminist Perspective* (Hants: Marshall Morgan & Scott, 1983), 41-44.

382 Sebastian kappen, *Jesus and Culture*, op. cit., 18.

lips. At Jesus time, the purity became just the superficial reality and was just performed by the high class for their gain and name. While speaking about Sabbath Jesus very clearly told that laws of purity are made by man and thus tradition should not take us off but there should be real commitment behind it (Mk.2:27). In this regard, Jesus demands love and justice which becomes the deciding factor for our purity and commitment. Thus, the source of defilement was unlove and injustice.[383]

## 5. Temple Cleaning

The attack on temple (Mk. 11:15-18) signified a radical cultural change, a total revolution in the religious and social set-up, ideas and arrangements. The temple had enormous revenues, supported many priests and levities who served it, and was a centre of Israel's social system and a symbolic centre of religious ideology. This was controlled by dominant class. Thus, the attack on the temple was an attack on the entire religio-political and cultural structure. Jesus saw the temple and class structure as the main source of oppression and the chief obstacle to the realization of the Kingdom. Jesus attack on the temple shows a way for reforming the religious and social set up which was caught up with class system. This cleansing also portrays the quest of Jesus for the equality of people and love for God.

## Implication of the Jesus' Counter Culture Movement

In the life and message of Jesus we witness the emergence of new force in history for the liberation of man which is constructive. For those who have encountered him, he represents the most powerful and authentic expression for man's striving fullness of being. As a quester after freedom he can be a source of light and inspiration to the millions in India who are groaning under the weight of organized oppression.[384] He kept the hope alive of the people for the liberation and he even pioneered the work for us so that we might follow the footsteps of Jesus. Hope grows only where the chains are broken, barriers overcome and walls pulled out. It dies

383 Sebastian Kappen, *Jesus and Culture*, op. cit., 20.

384 Sebastian Kappen, *Jesus and Freedom*, op. cit., 149.

out where man is not able to overthrow the oppressive structures of the present. The challenge given should be translated into action for the radical restructuring of society as Jesus did. Only ideology will not help unless and until the ideology is materialized by us. In order to make Jesus' message of liberation relevant to the exploited masses in India, the community must mobilize all its resources to quicken and nurture collective hope and fearlessly protest everything that makes a man less than a man, upholding love as the motive and end result of revolution.[385] Thus, the Church of today should be Open Community for all. The Church should be beyond churchist theology leaving aside the differences and trying to find the similarities rather than differences for the development of new egalitarian humanity which Jesus also aimed.

## Conclusion

**Martin Robbe** sees Christianity's emergence as a protest against the class society and its injustice. **Machovec** locates Jesus' counter –cultural thrust in his concern for the whole human person, as well as in his teaching that the future of our Earth depends upon our action and not on nature or fate. [386] This brief survey is enough to show that Jesus' teaching and practice was subversive of the value system of his day and that what he initiated was nothing less than a counter-culture. Every counter-culture needs a community as its bearer. Jesus had called disciples in his time and at present he calls us who are his disciple to be the bearer of this counter-culture in our present context. Thus we can affirm that Jesus was the pioneer for the counter-culture movement.

---

385 Sebastian Kappen, *Jesus and Freedom*, op. cit., 175.

386 Samuel Rayan, op. cit., 138.

Chapter XIII

# Concept Salvation and Humanization Defined: M. M. Thomas

## Introduction

M. M. Thomas (1916-1996) was a versatile thinker and theologian who wrote on a wide range of issues, such as Asian revolution, Nation building, Political and Social changes, Secularism, Inter-faith dialogue and Ecumenism. In the history of contemporary Ecumenism M. M. Thomas belongs to those who have shaped not only the ecumenical theology of missions, but the ecumenical movement itself.[387] Theological reflection indeed was his primary passion. Most significantly, he has provided a theological framework for interpreting the many struggles of people for justice. He didn't wanted people to be passive but active and participative in the struggles for the upliftment and equality. The concept Salvation and Humanization are in dialectical relation. Thomas search of

387 Sunand Sumithra, *Revolution as Revelation: A Study of M. M. Thomas's Theology* (New Delhi: Theological Research and Communications Institute, 1984), 2.

understanding the Salvation was propelled by his conviction that Christians have to take up responsibility and should participate in struggle and group movements. The whole relation spells clearly the need of Christian participation in people's struggle. Before we look into these two main themes of Thomas's writing, we will try to quickly see his theological framework which would give us better understanding to view these themes.

## Theological Methodology

In Thomas understanding theology is living and dynamic. A living theology is always situational and contextual. This spells out two implications: one the theological task in Asia today involves a new evaluation of the classical and confessional theological traditions the Asian Churches have inherited from the West; second a deep involvement in the Asian situation is the condition of new theological renewal. Theology is living thing, having to do with our existence as Christian and as Churches.[388] Thomas says, "The Churches can't stand on the side-lines as spectators, but must involve themselves in contemporary Asian existence in solidarity with the human and spiritual struggles of the World..."[389] Thomas finally views that Theology is human oriented praxis: "every theology has an anthropological content inherent in it or derived from it..." [390]

Thus, theology is action oriented and demands our participation which is our responsibility. So in this context we will try to understand the theme: Salvation and Humanization and Participation in People's Struggle in M. M. Thomas's writings.

## I. Salvation and Humanization

In the thinking of Thomas, Salvation and Humanization have a dialectical relation and it can't be seen in isolation. The theological presuppositions with regard to the relation between the concept of

---

388 M. M. Thomas, *The Acknowledged Christ of Indian Renaissance* (Madras: Christian Literature Society, 1970), 314-315.

389 Ibid.

390 M. M. Thomas, *The Secular Ideologies of India and the Secular Meaning of Christ* (Madras: Christian Literature Society 1976), 193.

Salvation and the quest for the fuller humanity make explicitly clear that Thomas can't go along with those who assert that the message of the Gospel can be fully known in isolation from the human quest.[391] Thomas explained the importance of the relation between Salvation and Humanization for the communication of the Christians faith to the contemporary World. Thomas says:

> The crucial question raised in the theology of mission in the World today is that of the relation between the Gospel of Salvation and the struggles of men/women everywhere for the humanity, constituting as this does the contemporary context of the World in which the Gospel has to be communicated. The question, in other words, is that of the relation between Mission and Humanization.[392]

Thomas further says, "Humanization of our common life becomes a common concern, a common medium of communication, and even a common criterion for evaluation of the various meaning of Salvation".[393] Salvation remains eschatological, but the historical responsibility within the eschatological framework cannot but include the task of Humanization of the world of secular history. The mission of Salvation and the task of Humanization are integrally related to each other even if they can't be considered identical. Thomas very clearly states that, "but there is no reason why historical destiny of human being (anthropology) could not be the point of entry for the understanding of man's ultimate destiny in the purpose of God, that is his eternal Salvation".[394]

391 Hielke T. Wolters, *Theology of Prophetic Participation: M. M. Thomas Concept of Salvation and the Collective Struggle for fuller Humanity in India* (Delhi: ISPCK, 1996), 177.

392 M. M. Thomas, *Salvation and Humanization: Some Crucial Issues of the Theology of Mission in Contemporary India* (Madras: Christian Literature Society, 1971), 2.

393 M. M.Thomas, "Christology and Pluralistic Consciousness," *International Bulletin of Missionary Research* 10/3 (July, 1986): 106. cited by Hielke T. Wolters, in *Theology of Prophetic* Participation: M. M. Thomas Concept of Salvation and the Collective Struggle for fuller *Humanity in India* (Delhi: ISPCK, 1996), 181.

394 M. M. Thomas, *Salvation and Humanization*, op. cit., 8-9.

## Humanization in Pluralistic Situation

A close relation between Salvation and Humanization is conceived by Thomas when he says that Church's Missions is, "to make clear that Salvation is the spiritual inwardness of the true Humanization, and that Humanization is inherent in the message of Salvation in Christ".[395] Thus, the idea of Divine mission in historical development is not untheological. Thomas talking about the pluralistic situation says about path of Humanization. Thomas says, "one could take several ways of expressing the core of the Gospel..., but it is God's identification with human suffering rather than Paul's emphasis on atonement for human sin which has been crucial".[396] Thomas emphasizes the historical responsibility as the framework of pluralism because it posits Humanization and the questions related to the meaning of being human as the central theme of common concern in dialogue and action for those who are encountering common issue. In this regard, Thomas says:

> Missionary participation in the Humanization of the world should be characterized by constant awareness of the mystery of the death and resurrection of Christ... Its purpose is to make Christ known as the source of foundation of true Humanization. The glorified humanity of Risen Christ is to be realized not after death but within the historical process, not by isolated individuals but in society and to the cosmos.[397]

Thomas while speaking in 1977 at Juhnon Mar Thomas Memorial Lectures spoke about elements of humanism. He says 'Jesus' statement that Sabbath is made for man and not man for Sabbath shows that institutions of religion, society or state is made to help and develop the humanity of people. Jesus saw his mission of Salvation as consisting of proclaiming good news to the poor and liberating the captives and declaring the year of Universal freedom.

395 M. M. Thomas, *Salvation and Humanization*, op. cit., 10.

396 M. M. Thomas, *The Church's Mission and Post-Modern Humanism* (Tiruvalla & Delhi: Christava Sahitya Samithi (CCS) & ISPCK, 1996), 131.

397 M. M. Thomas, *Salvation and Humanization*, op. cit., 10.

So, the new humanity which God recreates in Jesus Christ recognizes no distinction of religion, culture, society or nature - the ultimate category is the human solidarity'.[398]

## The Concept of Salvation

Thomas concept of Salvation has been clearly defined by Thomas himself:

> God sent His Son into the World that the World through him might be saved (Jn.3:17). That in the life, death and resurrection of Jesus the Nazareth God has acted to save the World is the core of Christian Gospel. Mission could be defined as communication of this message of Salvation through Jesus Christ to the end that human may respond in faith and be saved.[399]

This description of the message of Salvation has few aspects. Firstly, Thomas roots his understanding of Divine Salvation in the life, death and resurrection of Jesus Christ. Secondly, the communication of message of Salvation requires understanding of the language of the human response in their struggle for humanity. Thomas mentions that missionary enterprise in early India was basically conservative but inspite of this they became bearer of social and cultural Humanization as their very approach to outcaste with the Gospel changed the spiritual foundations. Salvation in Christ became the source of new human fellowship at least at the religious worship and helped to remove the unequal social structure. Thus, Humanization in India was the preparation of the Gospel.[400] Thomas viewed that the concept of Salvation should be looked from the ecumenical point of view also. He says, "there is growing recognition today that the scope of Christ's Salvation is wide enough to cover personal, social and cosmic dimensions, that the victory Christ has wrought is not only over personal sins but also over principalities and powers of

398 M. M. Thomas, *Revolution in India and Christian Humanism* (New Delhi: Forum for Christian Concern for People's Struggle, 1978), 3.

399 M. M. Thomas, *Salvation and Humanization*, op. cit., 10.

400 Ibid., 16.

corporate life…" [401] Thomas cites Bangkok Missionary Consultation on Salvation Today in 1972,

> It is Salvation of soul and body, of individual and society, mankind and the groaning Creation. As evil works in both personal life and in exploitative social structures which humiliate humankind, so God's justice manifests itself both in the justification of the sinner and social and political justice… the comprehensive notion of Salvation demands of the whole of the people of God matching comprehensive approach to their participation in Salvation.[402]

## New Man, Jesus Christ as Prototype

In interpreting the Cross as the way of life for Human and God, and in making it sense of Christian message of Jesus Christ, Thomas sets up Jesus as the ideal of what man/woman should be, to be a true person. Thomas also affirms that Jesus Christ is redeemer and archetype human.[403] Thus, Jesus Christ is the bearer of new humanity who gives courage to human to withstand the challenges of the World. This approach to relate mission of Salvation and Humanization has been criticized by Peter Beyerhaus who saw in it, a shift of the center from God to human which replaces theology to anthropology.

In response to this Thomas gives three thoughts: firstly, regarding the relation of theology and anthropology. Thomas viewed that 'the ultimate framework is neither God nor man in the abstract, but Jesus Christ who is God - man or God for man or humanity of God. Secondly, in relation to Salvation history and World history he views that these two can't be separated. Thirdly, Sin and Salvation has say in the corporate life which expresses our relationship to human in corporate structures of family, caste nation and international. The Kingdom of resurrection life for both individual and community

401 M. M. Thomas, *Religion and the Revolt of the Oppressed* (Delhi: ISPCK, 1981), 5-6.

402 Pauline Webb, *Salvation Today* (London: SCM Press, 1974), 70 cited by M. M. Thomas in *Religion and the Revolt of the Oppressed* (Delhi: ISPCK, 1981), 6.

403 Sunand Sumithra, *Revolution as Revelation,* op. cit., 164.

does not start after death but it partially begins and is partially realized here and now'.[404]

## Secular Koinonia - Fellowship

Thomas takes Colossians Chapter 3 and brings the thought of new community which is valid to present new fellowship of mutual forgiveness created by Divine forgiveness in Christ expressed in the Eucharist and social koinonia of the Church as the foretaste of true human community as the essential Gospel. The nature of this koinonia in Christ is that it transcends all communities defined by nature, culture and even ideology and religion and open for inter-personal communication with each other. In this process, closed communal life based on idolatry of communal self-identity and pursuit of communal self interest gets broken, opening it to a vision of their common humanity and their relatedness to each other in mutual forgiveness, justice and love.[405] Thomas talks of the three levels of koinonia in Christ: first the koinonia of the Eucharist community of the Church, itself a unity of diverse people accepting the Person of Jesus, second, a larger koinonia of dialogue among people of different faiths inwardly being renewed and third, those who are involved in power politics struggling for new society based on secular anthropology informed by the agape of Cross.[406]

## Dialogue with Hinduism on Humanization

Thomas believed that the relation between Salvation and Humanization that is between the ultimate destiny of human and his/her historical destiny, which is fundamental in Christian thinking is also fundamental issue debated within all the religions and in secular movements. So Humanization is the most appropriate theme for the point of entry for any dialogue with Hinduism and other secular

404 M. M. Thomas, *Salvation and Humanization*, op. cit., 7-9.

405 M. M. Thomas, *The Church's Mission and Post-Modern Humanism,* op. cit., 132.

406 M. M. Thomas, *Risking Christ for Christ's Sake* (Geneva: WCC Publications, 1987), 119.

movements.[407] The relation between faith and history in the Christ event needs further exploration in the Hindu context. Hinduism from both social and spiritual level deals with the question of the relation between human's ultimate spiritual destiny and the regeneration of human society. Both, Gandhiji and Swami Vivekananda spoke about having principle in common rather than historical person because Salvation in Hinduism is centered on principles.[408] But,Thomas says one of the tasks of theology of mission is to restate the significance of the historicity of the Person of Jesus within the essential core of the message so that historical human existence can acquire a positive relation to our eternal Salvation.

## Dialogue with Secularism on Humanization

Thomas in line with dialogue sees relevance of Christian dialogue with Indian Secularism which would give adequate spiritual basis for a secular society. Thomas says, 'dialogue between Christianity and secularism at the inter-faith level acquires an active co-operation between them in the Humanization of the structures of society and state'. Thomas views that biblical categories and forms of language are not universally intelligible enough for the modern secular person, without looking into the newness of the given situation. A theology of mission should help the Christian Church to participate in social praxis. The form of the Church is a question of radical importance in this secular age. Thomas opines that 'secularization has till some extent reduced the importance of Church and thus in India it is important to ponder on the Christian religious values by redefining them to make relevant for the contemporary World'.[409] So, we need a new pattern of combining Christian self-identity and secular solidarity with all human.

## II. Participation and People's Struggles

Thomas a man of vision and practice has enlightened Christendom and had indeed widened the Christian thinking. Thomas very clearly

---

407 M. M. Thomas, *Salvation and Humanization,* op. cit., 20.

408 Ibid., 27-28.

409 Ibid., 59-60.

while talking on the liberation praxis spells out three basic human rights: the right to bread, the right of equality and the right of every group and person to spiritual self determination. He says, 'for the weaker section of the society freedom means to struggle for their self identity, self development and self determination. For the poor and oppressed, it opens up the path of their liberation through their own organized efforts. This is a collective right of groups of people to resist social, cultural and religious dominations as well as economic exploitation'.[410] While giving the convocation address at the Union theological Seminary in New York in 1967, Thomas said, "The understanding of the Gospel as new humanity in Christ probably will emerge only as theologians participate with others in the struggle for Humanization of society".[411] As I read Thomas I find that he is to some extend very bold to view that without the militancy of people from below expressing itself in pressures for total revolution of economic, social and cultural patterns, no efforts could be of great use.[412] He is mentioning that there should be struggle within and people should realize the need of it. Thus, we participate in helping them.

## Concern for Social Justice

Thomas viewed that we as Christian enter into day to day struggle with a fundamental concern of justice which challenges us for social justice. Thomas mentions that Martin Luther King in his discussion of the Black power violence clarifies that participation in political power and processes is the essence of human dignity. He mentions that there are two types of human rights: one is the people's right, the right of tribal peoples, rights of dalits, of women and rights of peoplehood of certain section of society; and two within each people, the

---

410 M. M. Thomas, *Revolution in India and Christian Humanism,* op. cit., 4-6.

411 T. M Philip, *The Encounter Between Theology and Ideology: An Exploration into the Communicative Theology of M. M. Thomas* (Madras: Christian Literature Society, 1986), 132.

412 M. M. Thomas, *Religion and the Revolt of the Oppressed*, (Delhi: ISPCK, 1981), 58.

rights of each people. Thus, in this sense we are concerned with the fundamental rights of human person for freedom and equality.[413] Thomas speaking of Kuncheria Pathil states that "it is demanded by the Church that in the face of oppressive situation of the people, it must organize itself into people's movement for liberation cutting across the boundaries of religion, caste and culture, making it an open Church with flexible structures".[414] It is thus the urgency of the time that people look for freedom and justice for all humanity.

## Technology and People's Struggle

Thomas mentioning about the Amsterdam Conferences tells that they spelt out the meaning of justice in technological society in two directions, both emphasizing real participation of people in centers of power which affects their life. First, by seeing responsible society as criterion and goal of just society. Thus, it asked the Churches to reject the idea of communism and capitalism. The other focus was the supremacy of people over purely technical considerations. Thomas says, "The danger of technology was that it would undermine the natural foundations of society in family, neighborhood and craft.[415] The present attitude of poverty and famine is the result of the impact of technology. Technology can be used to exploit poor or to meet the basic needs of the poor. But, it depends upon the moral decision of the society.

Thomas while talking about the MIT Boston Conference on Faith, Technology and the Future says that it has deepened the issue of this debate. One of the focuses was the ethics of appropriate technology. It demands that technologies should be appropriate to international and social justice which liquidates poverty and enhances human work as vocation everywhere, enabling people's participation in decision making processes of economic, social and political life within a proper natural environment.[416] As we survey the World situation today Thomas opines that there are two crucial struggles

---

413 M. M. Thomas, *The Church's Mission and Post-Modern Humanism,* op. cit., 78.

414 Ibid., 135.

415 M. M. Thomas, *Religion and the Revolt of the Oppressed*, op. cit., 31.

416 M. M. Thomas, *Religion and the Revolt of the Oppressed*, 34.

of the poor and oppressed. The major concern is the struggle of the people in all parts of the World, more especially in Asia, Africa and Latin America, to overcome their extreme poverty. The other is the struggle for racial justice, which is a World wide phenomenon in its scope. In India, several groups who were marginalized by the traditional societies are awake and are creating a situation of crisis. The outcastes, the tribals, and the women have had little participation in the traditional power structures of Indian societies. So, these people are not asking bread merely but bread, work and fellowship as indices of real social participation.[417]

The Nairobi Assembly in 1975 talked about the struggle against oppression and injustice inevitably necessitates confrontation with power and the handling of power. Churches have in the past underestimated the dimensions of these aspects even when they have marginally recognized them. Nairobi, 1975, also added that 'the political struggle against poverty must be struggle which the people themselves must wage. If anybody wants to help, they should fight not just for the people but with them. It is through such struggles that manipulated masses become people'.[418] Even the world Council of Churches views that the struggle in the process of liberation must be accepted and should be understood as necessary. As we look into all these responses, Thomas endeavor in the struggles of people, it is right to discuss the Christian participation in the ongoing struggles of human as individual and by large in society.

## Church & Christian Participation

The whole ecumenical setting calls for a necessity of people's awakening, people's organization and people's participation for the struggle of social justice. Thomas mentions that the most recent statement of WCC, Church's concern for participation in development is "Towards a Church in Solidarity with the Poor". It vehemently expressed that the struggle in the process of liberation must be accepted. The Church should not run away from it but actively involve in the process of liberation. Thomas spells out one

417 M. M. Thomas, *Religion and the Revolt of the Oppressed*, 38.

418 Ibid., 49.

of the greater unity mantra: "participation in the struggle of Asian people's for the fuller human life in state, society and culture, in a real partnership with men/women of other faiths and no faiths, is the only context for realizing the true being of the Church and exercising the Church's ministry and mission". [419] It can be noted that either in the evangelistic mission of proclamation of Gospel or of Church's meaning social service and prophetic ministry, or the larger unity of the Church, has the real meaning within the context of participation and partnership. In this regard, Thomas recalls the view of Assembly of East Asia Christian Conference quoting:

> Christian people must go into every part of life of our people's, into politics, into social and national service, into the world of art and culture to work in real partnership with non-Christians and to be witness of Christ in all these realms.... It means also that each congregation must know that it is put in the world by the Lord as his representative and that it must therefore be chiefly concerned, not with itself, but with the world...[420]

## Participation along with People of Other Faiths

We very clearly find in the thoughts of Thomas that he persuaded the Churches to come out of their Christian ghettoes, Mission compound ideology and inward looking thought which is self based. Thomas says "As the whole World is awake to the task of building the human society and culture, a partnership in nation building between Christian and Non-Christian is the proper context of evangelism".[421] This demands from the Christian people that it must march forward not with any idea of controlling, but to serve humanity and in that process be a witness to Jesus Christ and his power which will enable

---

419 M. M. Thomas, *The Christian Response to the Asian Revolution* (London: SCM Press LTD, 1966), 104.

420 *Witness Together*, Being the official report of the Inaugural Assembly of the EACC, held at Kuala Lumpur, Malaya (14-24 May, 1959), cited by M. M. Thomas in *The Christian Response to the Asian Revolution* (London: SCM Press LTD, 1966), 104-105.

421 Ibid., 106.

human being to keep their humanness. So, Christians must involve themselves with others creating and promoting ideologies which are informed by Christian insight, and which can help people's struggle for justice.

In the context of today, Thomas says that participation is the part of prophetic ministry. So who participate in the struggle of people can be prophets and thus this demands from us commitment and courage. This prophetic ministry is based on love and service for the betterment of the humanity.[422] Thus, there is a fresh call for the Church to be prophetic being and loose out its timidity and face the challenges of the given context. Even though there will be constant tension between the Church and the Society but this tension can become creative by the active efforts of Church's participation.

One of the main point in this area of participation and people's struggle what Thomas brings in, is the concept of service which has become now the linking thread with the society and other faiths. The Christian participation can be of more fruitful if we join together with the secular World and other faiths in the development of society in the area of education, health and social services. And more over to this the pressing need is that social service should turn to be social action which would think of changing social structures. Thus, this co-corporation will lead for the renewal of the society which ultimately will be national building.

Thomas while addressing Sri Lanka Theological College challenged by saying that the new anthropology is needed as the basis of a more healthy process of development and modernization. The people those who are involved in the welfare of marginalized need to explore more the relation between the modernity and tradition to develop them. He also emphasized that Church must be prepared to stand by people when they struggle for the economy that gives priority to eco-justice and social justice rather than just economic growth.[423]

---

422 *Witness Together*, Being the official report of the Inaugural Assembly of the EACC, held at Kuala Lumpur, Malaya (14-24 May, 1959), cited by M. M. Thomas in *The Christian Response to the Asian Revolution* (London: SCM Press LTD, 1966), 108.

423 M. M. Thomas, *The Church's Mission and Post-Modern Humanism,* op. cit., 126-127.

## Evaluation and Conclusion

At the very outset it can be seen that there is an urge for the Gospel to be more social and liberative in nature. Yes indeed Gospel has been involved in the development of the social context but at the same time it had its own motives. The writings of M. M Thomas is challenging and even sometimes shaking the foundations of faith. Thomas challenges us to rethink the concept of Christian Mission in the changing context. He challenged that Church should identify with the World and participate in its struggle for Human rights, Social justice and World community and the setting of such participation is essential condition for the Church's renewal in Mission. He is very clear that the theology and anthropology should go hand in hand. Mission should not detach from the World but attach so that its purpose gets fulfilled.

Thomas hopes that through participation in struggles for the restoration of humanity, and dialogue with ideologies of such participation, it will be possible to convey the Christian concern for the Creation of a genuine humanism and Jesus Christ as its goal to contemporary Indian cultural milieu. Thomas keeps a dialectical tension between the horizontal and vertical dimensions when he talks about the relation of Salvation and Humanization. Our human concern is surely related with the spiritual aspect of life. So, as one takes part in the people's struggle it is not just the struggle of others but it is more or less struggle within us. Thus, in this context the reality of the fellowship of Christ's new humanity is present and active in the life and thought of men/women of other religions and secular faiths. Thus, Thomas very clearly calls for a secular koinonia (fellowship) so that there will be harmony and we might learn from each other.

In the pluralistic context, where many religions and faiths exists, Thomas concept of secular koinonia is great and challenging. His theological concept of participation and dialogue gives us the impetus for doing theology in more meaningful way. Moreover to that it gives us space to accommodate other faiths and mutually stand together on one platform without negating the other. Thomas calls Church for a greater participation and challenges it to have prophetic participation by shunning the timidity and standing against all the oppressive elements of the Society or even Church. His theology is not just a theoretical concept but a realistic thought which talks about liberation of poor, tribal, dalit and women. Thus, there could be no exaggeration that he could be called a pioneer in the theology prophetic participation. I think there is a proto call for the Church to leave its four walled ideology and move out to the World, for Jesus himself has called to be a witness of his love, service and humanity.

Chapter XIV

# The Basics of Tribal Religion and Culture

## Introduction

Next to Africa, India has the largest tribal population in the World. There are 360 different tribes (sub-tribes being many more) speaking more than 100 languages in India with the population of around 68 million people, which constitute about 8.10 % of our country's total population according to 1991 census.[424] Some still primitive and others are developing, and even few are well developed and organized. Each tribe has its own distinctive culture, language, lifestyle and religious believes. At the same time, each of them has their own problems due to their socio-economic situation and their religious and cultural experiences. Since tribals of India have been very responsive towards Gospel, it gives us challenge to understand their culture and religion in a better way. In order to have a better

424 R. C.Verma, *Indian Tribes Though the Ages* (New Delhi: publication division, Ministry of Information and Broadcasting, Govt. of India, 1995), 9.

understanding we need to first acquaint ourselves with the term tribal, their setting and then study the tribal religion and their culture with special reference to North Eastern India.

## Defining Tribals

India is a vast land of thousands ethnic groups classified into tribes, castes and communities. They represent a diversity of religions and cultures. The oldest inhabitants of the land are officially classified as Scheduled Tribes (S.T) popularly known as Adivasis implying original inhabitants. Etymologically, the term tribe derives its origin from the word tribes meaning three divisions: firstly for Romans, the tribe was a political division. Secondly, in Western World and India, tribe was highest political unit comprising of several districts having a definite geographical area. The territory under the domain of a particular tribe was generally named after it. It is believed that India derived its name Bharat from the mighty Bharat tribe same as Mizoram (Mizo tribe) etc,.[425] Thirdly, in Europe with the growth of nationalism, the term tribe came to denote a race of people within the given territory.

It is very difficult to define the term tribal but in general, a tribe may be describes as an indigenous homogenous unit, speaking common language, claiming a common ancestry, living in a particular geographical area, backward in technology, loyally observing social and political customs based on kinship.[426] Tribe in the dictionary of anthropology is defined as, "a social group, usually with a definite area, dialect, cultural homogeneity and unifying social organization. It may include several subgroups, villages. The families or small communities making up the tribe are liked through economic, social, religious, family, or blood ties.[427] D. N. Majumdar says, "A tribe is a social group with territorial affiliation, ruled by tribal officers,

425 R. C.Verma, *Indian Tribes Though the Ages* (New Delhi: publication division, Ministry of Information and Broadcasting, Govt. of India, 1995), 2.

426 Consultation Findings, "The Mission of the Church and the Development of Tribal Communities in India Today", *Religion and Society* 9/4 (December, 1962): 81.

427 K. L.Bhowmik, *Tribal India: A Profile in Indian Ethnology* (Calcutta: The world press private ltd. 1986), 1.

hereditary or otherwise, united in language, and dialect, following tribal beliefs, and traditions & customs".[428] There are three major groups of tribal in India: firstly, those who are Munda language family like Santhals, the Mundas, and the Saoras etc. Secondly, those who belong to the Monkhamer language family like Boros, the Nagas, the Mizos, the Garos and others. Thirdly, those who belong to Dravidian language family, like the Gond, the Kui, the Oraons etc. These tribals have roots in their own culture and civilization.

According to Dr. B. S. Guha, tribal people lived fairly well in three zones. In the North and the North East zone there were tribes such as Bhotia, Tharu, Gurung, Limbu, Aka, Mishmi, Dafla, Kachari Garo, Khasi, Naga, Mizo and Lepcha. In the Central zone we find, Santhal, Munda, Oraon, Ho, Bhumij, Kol, Kharia, Bhuiyan, Gon, Bhil, and Kond. The Southern zone contains tribes such as Chenchu, Toda, Kadar, Badaga, Kota, Uraili, Pulaya and many more.[429] Out of this 87% of Scheduled Tribe population is concentrated in the central belt covering 8 States of Madhya Pradesh & Chattisgarh, Orissa, Bihar & Jharkhand, Maharashtra, Gujrat, Rajasthan, Andhra Pradesh and West Bengal. About 10 % in the North Eastern region and about 3% in other states. Madhya Pradesh and Chattisgarh have the highest concentration of 23% of total scheduled tribe population of India. Thus, in brief S. C Dube gives the basic characteristics of tribals: 1. their roots in the soil date back to a very early period. 2. They live in relative isolation of the hills and the forests. 3. Their sense of history is short and their history of five to six generation tends to get merged in mythology. 4. They basically base on land and agriculture.[430]

428 D. N. Majumdar, *Applied Anthropology in India*, edited by L.P.Vidyarti (Delhi: Kitab Mahal, 1984) 86.

429 B. S. Guha, "The Indian Aborigines and their Administration", *Journal of Asiatic Society* (Science), Vol.17 (1951), cited by Bijitendra Mohan Mitra, *Codification of Tribal Customary Laws* (Kolkata: The Indian Anthropological Society, 2003), 57.

430 S.C. Dube, *Tribal Heritage of India: Ethnicity, Identity and Interaction,* Vol.1 (New Delhi: Vikas Pub., House, 1977), 2.

## The Settings of Tribal

In the past, tribals lived in isolation untouched by outside influences in the socio-religio-cultural structures. As a result of this isolation they could maintain and develop their own separate cultures, social and political organizations and religious beliefs. Following is the situation of the tribals in brief:

**Social setting:** As isolated groups, the tribes developed their own social systems of organization based on families' ties and blood relationship. In such society, there was great deal of equality whether between women and men, heads of families, or clans or tribes. Owing to their common lives in tribe, they developed an intense loyalty to their own tribal group. In individual as well as in collective thinking, the tribe had pride in itself and all were greatly concerned about the preservation of its identity. The tribes of North East India are very much free from many of the social evils of the larger Indian society. They have no cast system and the associated evils like untouchability or social inequality; they do not have dowry system as it prevails in the larger Indian society.[431] However, tribal society is also changing rapidly since they are in contact with the outside world. S.C. Das says, "Christianity has not caused any serious imbalance in the social order of the tribes, because, Christianity has not disturbed in any way the traditional social framework."[432] He carries on to say that conversion to Christianity has made North Eastern India closer to greater Indian culture.

**Economical Setting**: The main occupation of the tribal people was agriculture and this necessitated a firm attachment to the land. Each family produced enough food for itself, and due to their simple way of life, there was no accumulation of wealth. This perhaps accounted for their classless and casteless society.[433] Their chief cultivation was rice, fruits, raised cattle, goats, pigs etc. they used fishing and hunting equipments as bow and arrow, spears and

---

431 S. T. Das, *Tribal Life of North- Eastern India: Habitat, Economy, Customs and Traditions* (Delhi: Gain Publishing House, 1986), 31.

432 Ibid., 34.

433 Consultation Findings, op. cit., 83.

guns. The economical problems are of landlessness, land alienation, indebtness, backward agricultural practices and so on.

**Cultural Setting:** Owing to simple life, unaffected by complex thinking, to the purity of belief in the existence of Supreme Being and immortality of soul, nourished and developed amidst the varied beauties and harmony of nature. Their music, dancing, games and festivals express their way of life in many ways. The festivals were generally multi-purpose in character like it may be for religious worship, for social intercourse and many times it even became a political affair. Thus, many of their cultural activities are centered on their religion.

## The Tribal Religion

Tribals are said to be deeply religious in their own way. Their religious life does not make distinction between the sacred and secular, spiritual and physical, heavenly and earthly; all these together constitute wholeness of life. But, it is often believed that the tribal doesn't have religion of their own as such: they believe only in spirits and practice strange rites and ceremonies in their spirit worship. So their religion is branded as animist. Some others think that their religion is characterized as the primary stage of undeveloped religion, so it is called primitive religion or primal religion. But, all these terms are inadequate and derogatory. The tribal religion is much more than a primal or primitive religion.[434] Thus, this should be called as traditional tribal religion or traditional indigenous religion. A .Wait Longchar says, "The tribal religion is basically a community religion. To be truly human is to belong o the whole community, including the ancestors and Creation, and to do so involves the active participation in the beliefs, ceremonies, ritual and festivals of the community".[435]

---

434 Renthy Keitzar, *In Search of Relevant Gospel Message* (Guwahati: Christina Literature Centre, 1995), 84.

435 A Wati Longchar, *The Traditional Tribal Worldview and Modernity* (Jorhat: N. Limala, 1995), pp. 7-8.

## Features of Tribal Religion

Experiences of certain day to day sudden happenings, of diseases, death have lead tribal people to believe in a world other than the material world, i.e., in the invisible spirit-world or supernatural power. There are some main features of the tribal religion which we see in brief.

- Tribal religion have the believe in the **Supreme Being/ High God**, who is the Creator and sustainer of the Universe. All the ritual sacrifices, and festivals are observed to direct piety towards the Supreme God (SinghBonga for Munda people). Most tribals have a masculine name for the Supreme God. But, there are some tribals who have both, masculine as well as feminine name for God.[436]
- Another peculiar feature of tribal religion is that, it is basically a **community religion.** Human belongs to the whole community, including the ancestors and Creation. In tribal religion an individual's life and community life is inseparable. Belief and action go together and without this we can't understand religion. Tribal religion does not have a founder of a reformer. The tribal religion is not centered in a great person rather the religion is centered on Earth/ Creation. Thus everything is interwoven very closely.[437]
- The other feature of tribal religion is that the tribal religion doesn't have a **sacred scripture or scripture** like other religion. The religious ethos is contained in people's heart, minds, oral history and rituals. In a sense, people themselves are living scriptures and Creation declares the Supreme Being. They have myths and legends, folktales and stories in which the whole of their religious ethos are embodied. Thus, myths become the scripture for the tribal people. Myths convey profound religious feeling

---

436 Yangkahao Vashum, "Sources For Studying Tribal Theology", in *Tribal Theology: A Reader*, ed., Shimreingam Shimray (Jorhat: Tribal Study Centre, 2003), 68.

437 A Wati Longchar, *The Traibal Religious Traditions in North East India: An Introduction* (Jorhat: Eastern Theological College, 2000), 4-5.

and religious truth. They tell about God, spirits, and their relation with human being and Creation. They tell how human beings understand themselves, their life realities and their relationship with God and Creation. Thus, myth is a true story.[438]

- Among Tribal **animism** is also common feature. For them all spots and places are holy as they are seats of spirits. Animals, plants, trees, ponds, rivers, stones, hills or mountains are abodes of spirits. All tribes may be Santhal, Munda or Oraon or Mikirs or Garos or Nagas believe in spirits in some form. The Nagas move around their village with a big stone with the belief in the existence of certain spirit in the stone.[439] A tribal believes in four categories of spirits related to men: they are protective spirits, the benevolent spirits present every where, Evil or malevolent spirits which cause diseases and death, and ancestral spirits which are good in nature.
- Another feature of tribal religion is **worship of nature**. Sun, Moon and Earth are considered to be Creator or supreme power. In middle India, Santhals, Mundas, Hos, and others identify Sun as Sing Bonga, i.e., Supreme God. In the Himalayan region, the Garos consider the Sun, Moon and Stars as spirits placed in the heavens for ruling the region.
- Apart from the nature as whole the tribal people have also cognated themselves with the animals and plants in the form of **totems**. Totemism is a common feature of the tribal people of India and most of them believe in their mysterious relation with some plants, etc., they have some totemic objects and respect them.[440]
- **Taboo** is another feature of the tribal people. Some regard taboo as holy dread, an objectified fear of the demonic

438 A Wati Longchar, *The Traibal Religious Traditions in North East India: An Introduction* (Jorhat: Eastern Theological College, 2000), 69.

439 L. P. Vidyarthi & B. K. Rai, *The Tribal Culture of India* (New Delhi: Concept Pub., Comp., 1985), 239-40.

440 Ibid., 243.

power thought to be concealed in the tabooed object. The religious side of taboo is to keep things in order and prevents to be irreligious. The tribal believe that if taboo is violated then it may result in disaster. The sema Naga have *genna* as a parallel of taboo and chini of forbidden. A person killed by tiger is *genna.* His whole things become *genna* to people. A breach of law would bring on entire society Divine wrath. So, it is evident that the religious belief also exists in the form of taboos.[441]

- **Magic** is an integral part of tribal religion. Natural events, dangers, inadequate technical means leads to belief in magical practices. All the tribes have some or the other magical practices. Mudas go to top of hills and throw down stones of all sizes, so that rain may come in lieu of sound. Khnods believe in human sacrifice for rain. People believe magic is effective in dealing with mystical powers. So magical belief among tribals is strong, because it helps in controlling an epidemic, making rain, curing an ailing person etc.
- **Ancestor worship** is another important feature of the tribal religion. Through ancestors worship man acquires powers of far reaching and compulsive kind beyond his capacity. Tribals firmly believe in the idea that the spirits of the dead ancestors have power to decide their destiny and so they observe all the rites.[442] The spirits of the ancestors are called and worshiped annually or occasionally. Among Nagas, Mithun ceremony is very important. It is totally dedicated to spirits of ancestors. A mithun is sacrificed in the name of dead ancestor for their prosperity. The Mizos conceive that after the death of a person his spirit proceeds towards the Rih lake. It however, soon returns and resides near the home or village for about three months. It is therefore customary, when the family its for the meal it keep one seat vacant or some cooked food is kept near the

441 L. P. Vidyarthi & B. K. Rai, *The Tribal Culture of India* (New Delhi: Concept Pub., Comp., 1985), 244.

442 Ibid., 245.

house for ancestral spirit.[443] Later on after three months the farewell ceremony is done.

## The Tribal Culture

Tribals are well known for their rich traditional heritages. The traditional heritages include the past and the present, socio-cultural tradition, customs, and even religious practices. These traditional practices include myths and legends, folktales and stories, wisdom and proverbs, morals, songs etc. These cultural traditions existed and are transmitted orally from generation to generation. Renthy Keitzar describes the oral tradition of the tribal people as the unwritten "Prime Bible".[444] Each tribe in India has its own cultural distinctiveness. This cultural distinctiveness is related to their world view, customs, social structures and life styles. Tribals have a set of social and cultural principles based on social justice and kinship relations.

Tribal life is characterized by communitarianism, the principle of selfless love and concern for the welfare of community basically characterising the social and cultural life of tribal community. This governing principle of the tribal society is known as ***sobaliba*** in Ao-Naga and ***thawmnhaihna*** in Mizo.[445] It is s social ethical principle of the tribal community, which provides the basis for a communitarian society to exist and function effectively. This spirit of altruism may very well be described as the philosophical and ethical foundation of a communitarian society. They lead a life of sharing and caring, justice and honesty, simplicity and truthfulness. The welfare of the community takes precedence over all other things.

Another cultural practice of the tribal people that is of paramount importance is the system of 'bachelor's dormitory', which is widely known among Nagas as ***morung*** system and as ***zawlbuk*** among the Mizos. It may be rightly described as the cultural institution of the tribal community. This morung system has multiple functions. It is the cultural training center where the youngster are taught and

443 L. P. Vidyarthi & B. K. Rai, *The Tribal Culture of India* (New Delhi: Concept Pub., Comp., 1985), 246.

444 Renthy Keitzar, *In Search of Relevant Gospel Message*, op. cit., 85.

445 Yangkahao Vashum, "Sources for studying Tribal Theology", in *Tribal Theology: A Reader*, ed., Shimreingam Shimray (Jorhat: Tribal Study Centre, 2003), 70.

trained in all kinds of skills. It is the custodian of culture, traditions and values of the tribal community.

## The Tribal world View

In order to understand well the tribal culture we also need to understand well the tribal world view. God reveals and mediates through different cultures. Plurality is the nature of God and affirmation of plural nature of God is holistic. The study of tribal can be meaningful, transforming and liberating only when we put our self into their thinking perception of reality. Without the study of tribal world view there can be no proper understanding of tribal culture. In the tribal world view the land, Creation is the foundation for understanding the tribal people's culture, identity, personhood, religion and ethos.

- For the tribals, every creature is an active participant in the Divine has a measure of sensitivity and enjoys a certain degree of autonomy and freedom. Animals are considered to be as enfolders of Universe into a reality.
- For the tribals, the land is life. The land is the source of origin, nourishment, support, identity, and are considered to be sacred.
- In the tribal world view, the Supreme Being is organically related to all creatures. Without Creation/land the Supreme Being ceases to be Creator and Sustainer.
- The tribals perceive humanity an integral part of a macro-organism. Humanity relayed to Creation not in hierarchical sense, but as family members.
- The tribals do not have myths and symbols where humanity alone is saved while others segments of Creation are destroyed.
- Even the idea of sin is perceived organically. Sin has to do with real life situations and it can never be understood in abstract metaphysical terms.

- The tribals maintain a high reciprocal use of natural resources.[446]

## Evaluation and Conclusion

The social oppression and economic exploitation of the tribal people in India is of great concern. In order to understand the religion of tribal, we need to understand culture and in order to understand culture we need to understand their religious concepts. Thus, these both in many areas are interwoven. Nirmal Kumar Bose says, "Christianity has undoubtedly brought the message of richer life, a wider companionship and a new sense of dignity to converts".[447] It is very clear that missionaries have played a great part in helping the tribal people to overcome social oppression and economic exploitation. In my opinion, the culture of tribals are of great dignity and we need to appreciate and use it for the liberative purpose. Church is the agent of social justice and thus it should work according to this line. The communication of the Gospel if done should be done in line with their culture and religious values. To affirm the values of tribal people, we can look into the attitude of Late Pandit Jawaharlal Nehru who had a life long interest in and love for the tribals of India. He spoke five points in concern with tribal:

1. People should develop along the lines of their own genius and we should avoid imposing anything on them. We should allow them to encourage their own art and culture in their own way.
2. Tribal rights on land and forest should be respected.
3. We should try to train and develop local people for the work.
4. We should not over administer these areas by many schemes.

446 A Wati Longchar, "The Need For Doing Tribal Theology", in *Tribal Theology: A Reader*, ed., Shimreingam Shimray (Jorhat: Tribal Study Centre, 2003), 8-13.

447 Nirmal Kuma Bose, *Tribal Life In India* (New Delhi: National Book Trust, 1971), 65.

5. We should judge results not by statistics or the amount of money spent but by the quality of human character that is involved.[448]

A creative interaction of Gospel and Culture is therefore necessary for developing a holistic approach for the better development. Our focus should be to serve at all level of life, and our approach should appeal to all who suffer, those who struggle for justice and human dignity and for all Creation. Thus, religion and culture of tribal go side by side and it would be hard to draw a separate between it.

448 M. M. Thomas & Richard W. Taylor, eds., Tribal Awakening (Bangalore: CISRS, 1965, cited by F. Hrangkhuma, "Christ and Tribal Culture", in *Christ and Culture*, eds., Jacob Kavunkal & F. Hrangkhuma, (Bombay: St. Paul's Press, 1994), 149.

Chapter XV

# Reservation Issue in Relation to Minority in India

## Introduction

India is a land of diversities, diversities in terms of socio-cultural patterns, economic formations, language dialect groups, religious communities etc. These diversities make this country unique and gives it a distinct flavor. India's existence as plural society has been institutionalized with the development of the Constitution of India in 1950. To reinforce cultural, linguistic, religious and tribal identities, the Constitution enshrines a framework of safeguards to protect fundamental, individual and groups rights of minority. As we begin our discussion on the issue of minority and reservation we will first define the concept of minority, and see the rights of minority in the light of United Nations Declaration and Indian Constitution. The second part of the paper will highlight the reservation issue, its origin and its current debate. Aim of this chapter is to make the readers understand the concept of minority and its relation to reservation policy (quota) in the light of given upheaval.

## I. Defining the term Minority

The Oxford dictionary defines minority, as 'a relatively small group of people differing from others in the society of which they are a part, in race, religion, language, political persuasion, etc.' or 'the state of having less than half of votes or being supported by less than half of the body of opinion.' Louis Wirth defines minority as follows, "a group of people, who because of their physical or cultural characteristics are singled out from the others in the society in which they live, for differential & unequal treatment and who therefore, regard themselves as objects of collective discrimination". [449] Claire Palley defines minority as, "Any racial, tribal, linguistic, religious, caste or nationality group within a nation state and which is not in control of political machinery of the state."[450] In Wikipedia encyclopedia minority is defined as, "a subordinate group that does not constitute a political dominant plurality of the total population of a given society. A sociological minority is not necessarily a numerical minority — it may include any group that is disadvantaged with respect to a dominant group in terms of social status, education, employment, wealth and political power."[451]

In socio-economics, the term minority refers to subordinate ethnic group understood in terms of language, nationality, religion and culture. Other minority groups include people with disabilities, unemployed, age minorities, gender and sexual minorities. In India we can see minority as Schedule Tribes, Schedule Caste, Other Backward Class, Dalits, Christians, Muslims, Buddhists, Janis, Sikhs, etc. India is not only the largest democracy in the World but it is also home for the largest minority. But, when the rights of minorities

---

449 Francis Nallappan, "Hindutva and the Minorities: Communalism and Discipleship," in *In the Shadow of the Cross*, edited by Joseph Mattam & Reuben Gabriel (Mumbai: St. Pauls, 2002), 148.

450 Claire Palley, "Constitutional Law and Minorities," in *Readings on Minorities: Perspectives and Documents*, Vol. I, edited by Iqbal A. Ansari (New Delhi: Institute of Objective Studies, 1996), 37.

451 "Minority Group", p. 1; http://en.wikipedia.org/wiki/minority,(1-07-06).

are threatened it is prudent to know the rights and affirm them.[452] The existence of minority in society implies the existence of a corresponding dominant group with higher social status and greater privileges. "Protection of minorities is the hallmark of a civilized nation. According to *Gandhiji* the claim of a country to civilization depends upon the treatment it extends to the minorities. *Lord Acton* added another dimension: the most certain test by which we judge whether a country is really free is the amount of security enjoyed by the minorities."[453]

## A. Rights and Freedom

One particularly controversial issue is the idea that minorities should be granted special privileges that the majority does not enjoy. The term "minority group" often occurs alongside a discourse of civil rights and collective rights which gained prominence in the 20th Century. We will see the UN decalrarion on minority and Indian Constitution on minority.

### 1. United Nations Declaration - 10th Dec. 1948

**Article I**: *All human being are born free and equal in dignity and rights. They are endowed with reason and conscience and should act towards one another in a spirit of brotherhood.*

**Article 2**: *Everyone is entitled to all the rights and freedoms set forth in this declaration, without distinction of any kind, such as race, color, sex, language, religion, political or other opinion, national or social origin, property, birth or other status.*[454]

452 Mohammad Imran Ali, "Legal Protection for the Minorities in India," *Legal News & Views* 19/10 (October, 2005), 10.

453 Soli J. Sorabjee, "Minorities: National and International Protection," in *Readings on Minorities: Perspectives and Documents*, Vol. I, edited by Iqbal A. Ansari (New Delhi: Institute of Objective Studies, 1996), 165.

454 Christian Conference of Asia, *No Place in the Inn: Voices of Minority peoples in Asia* (Tokyo: Christian Conference of Asia, 1979), 96.

## United Nations Declaration- 1992[455]

Inspired by the provisions of Article 27 of the International Covenant on Civil and Political Rights concerning the rights of persons belonging to ethnic, religious or linguistic minorities, the UN declaration came.

**Article 1:** *States shall protect the existence of national or ethnic, cultural, religious and linguistic identity of minorities within their respective territorial...*

**Article 2:** *Persons belonging to national or ethnic, religious and linguistic minotities have the right to enjoy their culture, to profess and practice their own religion, and to use their own language, withour any discrimination. They have right to maintain their own association.*

**Article 4:** Minority may exercise their full human rights without any discrimination.

**Article 5:** National policies nad programmes shall be planned for minorities.

## 2. Constitution of India[456]

Many of the human rights and freedom contained in the international bill of rights are guaranteed under the Indian Constitution, in Article 12-35.

**Article15:** Prohibition of discrimination on grounds of religion, race, caste, sex or place of birth. Special provision of advancement for minority is discussed.

**Article 17:** Abolition of Untouchability.

**Article 24:** Prohibition of employment of children in factories.

**Article 25:** Freedom of free profession, practice and propagation of religion.

---

455 Cited by Iqbal A. Ansari, ed., "UN Declaration on Minorities, 1992" in *Readings on Minorities*, Vol.I (New Delhi: Institute of Objective Studies, 1996), 311-313.

456 S. K. Ghosh, *Protection of Minorities and Scheduled Castes* (New Delhi: Ashish Pub., House, 1980), 127.

**Article 29:** Protection of interests of Minorities – no one should be denied of admission into any educational institution aided by state on the ground of religion, race, and caste language.

**Article 30:** Rights of minority to establish and administer educational institutions.

**Article 330:** Reservation of seats for SC and ST in the house of people

**Article 335:** Claims of SC and ST to services and posts.

Apart from this from this some sections of the Indian Penal Code[457], Personal laws and many Legislative Acts deal with the matters concerning minorities' human right and freedom. The present upheaval is because of the reservation issue which is increased from 22.5 to 49.5 overall (SC-15%, ST-7.5% and OBCs-27%).[458] In this context we will take up the reservation issue and try to evaluate it and develop a possible thinking.

## II. Reservation or Quota Issue

The scenes from the streets of Mumbai, Delhi and other big Indian cities have shocked India. The whole upheaval is because of the reservation policy which the government had amended and tried to implement. Since this reservation policy plays a vital role in vote bank it becomes very important to understand and know its background. Since it is a very complex situation it will be very hard to bring a verdict but both the side of discussion can be evaluated.

### A. History of Reservation or Quota System

Reservation for the SCs, the STs and the OBCs has been made under Article 15(4) of the constitution which empowers the State to make

457 The provision include under Indian Penal Code are: promoting violent attacks on ground of religion, race, language (Sec 153), injuring or defining a place of worship to insult the religion (Sec 295), outrage religious feeling (Sec 295A) disturbing religious assemblies and insulting religion (Sec 297) and promoting enmity between different groups (Sec 505 (2) and Sec 505 (3)). Cited by Mohammad Imran Ali, "Legal Protection for the Minorities in India," *Legal News & Views* 19/10 (October, 2005),11.

458 Udit Raj, "A Sure Pill for Progress," *Indian Current* 18/17 (23 April, 2006), 31.

any special provision for the advancement of socially or educationally. Under the Constitution of India in 1951, 15% educational and civil service seats were reserved for SCs and 7.5% for STs. This was under the influence of Poone Pact (1932).[459] In 1953, Government sets up first Backward Classes Commission, headed by Kaka Kalelkar. In 1963, the Supreme Court mandates reservation should not exceed 50% in any institution otherwise it would violate Article 15. The 93rd amendment introduced a new clause to Article 15. This new amendment made court a defender of the law, while laws are made in the Parliament.[460] This later led for the Mandal Commission.

## B. Mandal Commission

B. P. Mandal was an Indian Parliamentarian, who as chairperson of the Mandal Commission, which was commissioned in 1978 under Murarji Desai Government to consider action politics for the backward classes. The Commission Report was submitted in Dec 1980. It sought reservation for 27 per cent of all services and public sector undertakings under the Central Government and 27 per cent of all admissions to institutions of higher education for Other Backward Classes (OBCs). The percentage was over and above the existing 22.5 per cent reservation for SCs / STs. In Aug 1990, the then Prime Minister VP Singh assured its implementation in Government jobs. There were many self-immolations attempts, including that of Rajeev Goswami, a Delhi University student. It led to widespread protests, which finally led to his resignation.[461]

In the Northern States anti agitation have a bloody records. In 1977-1978 when Bihar Chief minister Karpoori Thakur suggested

459 V. T. Rajshekar, "Will not Caste annihilation demand make us enemy of caste-based reservation?," *Dalit Voice* 25/5 (March1-15, 2006), 6.

460 Aaditya Dar, "Mandal Exposed: Part II", (13th April, 2006) p. 3, http://mail.sarai.net/pipcrreader- list/2006-April/mail (01-07-06).

461 http://www.ndtv.com/homepage/mandal.htm; (01-07-06) see also Dipanjan Roy Chaudhury, "Another Quota Row," Indian Currents 18/17 (23rd April, 2006), 26.

backward reservation, 118 people lost their life in caste war. In 1990, 12 people were killed in Bihar and Uttar Pradesh.[462]

## C. Criteria to identify OBCs

The Mandal Commission adopted various methods and techniques to collect necessary data. The Commission adopted some criteria which could be grouped under three major headings: social, educational and economical in order to identify OBCs. **Social**: 1. Castes/Classes considered as socially backward by others. 2. Castes/ Classes which mainly depend on manual labor for their livelihood. 3. Castes/Classes where at least 25% female and 10% male above the State average get married at an age below 17 years in the rural areas. **Educational**: 1.Castes/classes where the number of children in the age group of 5-15 years who never attended the school is at least 25 % above the State average. 2. Castes/Classes where the student drop out in the age of 5-15 years is at least 25%. 3. Castes/Classes among whom the proportion of matriculates is at least 25% below the State level. **Economic:** 1. Castes/Classes where the average value of family assets is at least 25% below the State average. 2 Castes/Classes where the number of families in the kuccha houses is at least 25% above the state average. 3. Castes/Classes where the source of drinking water is beyond half kilometer for more than 50% of the households.[463]

In 1993, the Supreme Court upheld 27 per cent reservation for OBCs. The reservation came into effect in Sept 1993 after the recommendations were accepted.

## D. Mandal II

In Aug 2005, the SC abolished all caste-based reservations in unaided private colleges. On Dec 2005, the Lok Sabha passed the 104th Constitution Amendment Act 2005, rolling back the SC judgment. The new clause allowed reservations for SCs/STs and OBCs in private unaided educational institutions. The latest controversy erupted over

---

462 Inderjit Badhwar, "Mandal Commission: Dividing to Rule," *India Today* 15/17 (Sep.15,990), 99.

463 Dinkar Sakrikar, "The Mandal Commission Report," (August, 1994) p. 1-2 http://www.pucl.org (01-07-06).

the Government's proposal to introduce 27 per cent reservation for OBCs in Central Government-funded higher educational institutes like IITs and IIMs.[464] The recent agitation is attached with the reservation policy introduced by Human Resources Development Minister Arjun Singh of reservation of seat for OBCs of 27% in educational institutions is referred as Mandal II.

The oversight committee set up by the Government on implementation of reservation for OBCs in higher educational institutions may still take time. The committee is headed by Veerappa Moily which is working on the modalities of implementing 27% reservation for OBCs in the instructions of higher learning. Moily says, "Its mandate is to do that without harming the interest of general category students. This can be done by increasing seats, for which more infrastructures would be needed, a task which is not impossible to achieve by next academic year."[465] Leaders like V.P. Singh, Paswan, Sharad Yadav, Ramdoss, Sitaram Yechury and Chidambaram are for reservation and wants that it should be implemented in one go.[466]

## E. Debate: For/Against on Reservation

Groundwork for the quota system was laid in the Indian Constitution, which implemented reservations as an attempt to reduce inequality and make up for years of lower-caste oppression. There had been lot written for and against the reservation in India and outside India also. People have reacted in both the ways and still the protest goes on. Here, highlighted are some of the main points which can be a point of discussion.

### 1. In Defense of Reservation

Shailini Gera, a Hayward resident spoke, "we have to acknowledge caste-based inequality and I definitely think this is small step to

---

464 Suman K. Jha & Debashish Mukherji, "Don't quota me!," *The Week* 24/21 (April 23, 2006), 13.

465 "Interim Report on Quota", (June 30, 2006), p. 1 http://www.daijiword.com/news (01-07-06).

466 "Quotas now or never; says OBC lobby," *The Times of India* (Kolkata), 3 July 2006, 6.

acknowledge the inequality that exist."[467] The objective of reservation is not mainly to eliminate poverty but to bring closer warring groups with each other.

(a) Reservation in jobs is provided on the basis of **social and educational backwardness** and not on the economical conditions. A rich dalit is not socially equal to poor Brahmin. Reservation brings some respectability to the beneficiary. Reservation will also achieve social egalitarianism by breaking the psychological barriers of the backwards.

(b) The **concept of merit** is an abstract term. By and large the merit concept is perceived by the people in terms of marks obtained in the qualifying exams. No doubt it is an objective method for selection. But, the most important question is that SCs and STs are depressed, who where never allowed to have education for centuries. So, how can they all of sudden compete with main line.[468]

(c) Reservation is an integral part of the concept of social justice, which is meant to uplift the vulnerable sections, which are denied opportunities for years together. Peter Alphonse said, caste was the correct basis; inequality is reality; reservation was one of the ways to eliminate it.[469]

(d) Giving backward castes advantages in return of centuries of oppression is noble and just cause. Since the old Hindu order suppressed them on the basis of their genes, the present has to do patch up. Competition is only valid among equals. Those treated as unequal in the past should be given a more than equal status to make them eligible for an equal competition. Reservation is what a little we can do to correct age - old imbalances.[470]

---

467 Kimra Mcpherson, "Caste-based quotas in India spark protest," p.2, http://www.mercurynews.com (01-07-06).

468 Abhijeet Kumar, "Internal reservations for SC/ST," *Dalit Voice* 25/10 (May 16-31, 2006), 9.

469 "Reservation, Vital to achieving social justice", p. 1 http://www.hindu.com/2006/06/02/stories/20060217930800.htm (01-07-06).

470 Pankaj Pachauri, "The Great Debate: Mandal Commission," *India Today* 15/18 (Sep.16-30, 1990), 39.

(e) The Mandal Commission helps the backwards. India's past President K. R. Narayanan and current President A. P. J. Kalam are backward but are lifted high. Anil. K. Gupta says, "Reservation should be put in the larger social context. The thought should be for the poor. There are institutions where after being merit student also, poor people are not able to go because of money. The question is, should we go in for a system where the students of rich and poor study in the same school? If this happens the education quality will improve.[471]

## 2. Against Reservation

It is very well said that this whole issue in fact seems to be divide and rule. It was noticed in 1990 that one of the most alarming aspects of reservation is the drastic lowering of standards in the medical and engineering colleges.

(a) The people who oppose the reservation policy call it a murder of the merit. That means there is no value of education with merit. Because a person from quota can enjoy the same privileges being even buffoon. This really raises a question of quality and standard. The seat reserved in higher learning will dilute standards, bring down the student morale.

(b) The reservation will lead to brain drain which will empty India of its goods. Since the new India had been built on the education provided at institutes such as the IIT. This will show the chronic lack of qualified candidates.

(c) Some people argue that reservation at the University level won't work until India improves the primary and secondary school education. Of the 202 million children who enroll in the country's 1 million schools every year, barely 15% make it to high school and just half of those

471 Anil. K. Gupta, "Think about the poor," *The Week* 24/21 (April 23, 2006), 14.

to graduation.[472] Infosys Chief Mentor N. R. Narayana Murthy has asked Government to channel its money to develop primary education. He says, "Basic problem in the country is primary and secondary education level where we have not been able to enroll sufficient students from disadvantaged sections". Expanding the reservation is not the right solution. [473]

## F. Evaluation and Suggestions

The implementation of criteria of OBCs does not tackle the roots of backwardness in our society. The very criteria that have been used to define backwardness, like high incidence of manual labor, illiteracy, lack of drinking water sources, are real problems and they cannot be solved through the implementation of job reservations. The backwardness of these castes and communities, as pointed out before, is rooted in the very socio-economic structure of relations at the village level. Without touching those, backwardness and poverty cannot be eliminated.

Participatory economic growth: Is reservation the answer: Only around 7 per cent of the Indian population aged 17-23 years acquires a college degree. And out of these, only a small miniscule goes to the educational institutes of excellence. In fact, it can be safely assumed that those reaching the level of college education do belong to the creamy layer of society. The really disadvantaged are those who cannot even dream to acquire a college degree and these are people from all castes, but too poor to afford education. Since a majority of the Indian population would not benefit from reservation in education, it is a poor instrument to ensure participatory growth.

To my mind, the biggest moral objective for the framers of the Constitution of India was to ensure that caste; religious, linguistic and regional identities get merged within a larger national identity. Reservation is not a means to achieve this objective because it

---

472 Manjeet Kripalani, "Reservation rocks India's Boat," Business Week/(June 05, 2006), p. 3 http://inhome.rediff.com/money2006/june/05quota.htm (01-07-06).

473 Dipanjan Roy Chaudhury, "Another Quota Row," *Indian Current* 18/17 (April, 23, 2006), 25.

propagates these identities. This is probably why the framers of the Constitution of India put a timeline of 10 years on reservations in public jobs for SCs and STs. The Directive Principles call for education of all children below the age of 14 years. Not only has this objective not been met, but it has received little attention in public dialogue. This is an objective that needs to be met before reservation in higher education can play out its stated role.[474]

Going beyond the politics, the Union Government should push a good primary and secondary education for all by creating infrastructure in all districts of the country, then the affirmative action of reservation should follow. Quota should be implemented with the condition that institutions increase their total number of seats to correct imbalances. It is the duty of the Government to make provisions for a just society. Many castes are still marginalized and it seems that reservation is one of the way by which they can be brought to the mainstream and open job opportunities for the backward. It is indeed right of the every section of the society to have the higher education. But, I personally believe at least in the medical stream there should be strict standard maintained and there should be no compromise with the quality because it is the matter of life and death.

## Conclusion

India has witnessed the unprecedented scale of inter-community violence, especially between Hindus and Muslims (Christians, Buddhists and Sikhs have also suffered) discrimination based on religion is seen not only by various religious communities but some time it is through police or some legislative acts. The task before us to understand the dynamics of different religions in relation to other social forces and to build a national identity and consciousness. Since the issue of reservation is valid it should be accepted but the politics of it should be negated. Indeed reservation should be there but before we cry for it, the basic educational development should take place so that there are people to compete and than have a dignified life and position.

474 Shalabh Kumar Singh, "Reservation: The Real Reason," New Delhi, p. 2 (01-07-06).

Chapter XVI

# Creation and the Human Responsibility

## Introduction

Ecology in relation to Christian Spirituality and mission can be understood in diverse ways and in various contexts; but at the very core of the term it refers to that area of one's being, where there is the intrinsic connectivity with the Divine. We know that human beings comprise of the body, mind & soul or spirit and it is the amalgamation of these three faculties that constitute every individual. It is what makes a human superior to other Creation. Hence, one's spiritually can be understood as a kind of a life line, a matrix, which determines one's self which characterizes an individual, apart from the other physical and mental faculties which distinguishes human from other Creation. Here an attempt has been made to explore spiritually from an ecological perspective. In this endeavour, we will try and understand what ecology is, in relation to Christian spiritually and mission.The first part deals with the concept and meaning of spirituality and its relation with ecology. The second section reflects the side of Mission's spirituality. And lastly, understanding spirituality in handling Ecological concern and its implication to renew and reconstruct the world in the pattern of new humanity for a peaceful Co-existence with other creations.

## A. Concept and Meaning of Christian Spirituality and its Relation with Ecology

### A. 1. Concept of Spirituality

The word spirituality has its origin in the Latin word "*spirutualitus*" and is derived from the root in "*spiritus.*" The adjective "*spiritalis*" or "*spiritualis*" or the root "*spiritus*" are the Latin translations of the Greek word "*Pneuma*" and "*Pneumaticos*" found in 1 cor. 2:14. Spirituality is then that basic existential attitude that enables one to live concretely according to the spirit, in one historical situation.[475]

The Christian spiritual life is a serious response of man to the revelation of God's love in Christ and consists in the loving knowledge and service of God and one's fellow beings in the mystical body of Christ. For Joann Wolski Conn, the term "spirituality, refers to both a lived experience and academic discipline. For Christian, it means one's entire life as understood, felt, imagined, and decided upon in relationship to God, in Christ Jesus, empowered by the spirit". Further Juan Esquerda Pribet would elucidate that the word "Spirituality" indicates a 'life style', a 'life in the spirit' (Rom.8:9), a 'walking according to the spirit' (Rom. 8:4). This spirituality is a 'vision-thing' in virtue of which we understand our life, its mission and message. It is the warp and woof of our entire life, since its colours are seeing, hearing, speaking, praying, beliefs, intellectual position, life choices, moral options: it is present in what we support and affirm, in what we protect and deny and in our moral options. Basically, Christian spirituality is living according to the spirit, but it has to take place in concrete socio-historical context. It is the ever changing socio-historical context that gives birth to various schools

475 J. Ponnore, "A spirituality for Indian Missionaries in the third Millenium," *Vidyajyoti Journal of theological Reflection* Vol. 65 (2001), 260.

of Christian spirituality according to the specific needs of each situation.[476]

## A. 2. Meaning of Spirituality

According to some modern view, spirituality is used in three distinct ways in contemporary discourse: Firstly, it refers to a general human capacity for self-transcendence, for movement beyond mere self-maintenance or self-interest. This means that the human beings experiences a deep longing to reach beyond themselves, 'to be more and be able to do something more'. A person does this within the horizons of whatever one imagines or judges to be ultimate. Secondly, spirituality can refer to a religious dimension of life, to a capacity for self-transcendence that is actualized by the Holy, however that may be understood. And thirdly, spirituality can refer to a particular type of religious experience, such as Christian, Hindu or Muslim[477]

According to Aruna Gnanadason, "Spirituality is life in God. It is a qualitative life; nothing is left outside the touch of the spirit".[478]

Thus, spirituality in a simplified form can be understood as that arena in the human being where there is pure and exclusive union with God which enables us to perceive all that is around us from different perspectives and responding to the Divine presence in every nature of the Universe.[479]

## A. 3. Relation between Spirituality and Ecology

The Earth is our origin, our nourishment, our support, our guide, then spirituality itself is Earth-derived. If there is no spirituality in

---

476 J. Ponnore, "A spirituality for Indian Missionaries in the third Millenium," *Vidyajyoti Journal of theological Reflection* Vol. 65 (2001), 260.

477 Susan Rakoczy, *In Her Name: Women Doing Theology* (Picter Maritzherg: Chester Publication, 2004), 375.

478 Aruna Gnanadasan, *Theology of Humanhood* (Delhi: ISPCK, 1986), 67.

479 Carmelita Usog, "Women's spirituality for justice" *Ecclesia of women in Asia: Gathering the voices of the silence*, edited by Evelyn Monteiro & Antoinette Gutzler, (Delhi: ISPCK, 2005), 235.

the Earth, than there is no spirituality in ourselves. The human and the Earth are totally implicated Earth in the other.[480]

An attempt to restore the relationship of God-Human-Nature, to heal the wounds inflicted on the Earth calls us to realize that ecological justice is necessarily tied up with social justice. There can be no saving of the plant Earth, without tackling the basic issues of justice. When justice is perverted, misinterpreted as justice for a few, resulting in accumulation of wealth, greedy spending of natural resources, love of consumerism, the whole Earth suffers along with humanity.[481]

## B. A Mission Understanding

### B. 1. Ecological Spirituality

That greatest of Christian saints, Francis of Assisi, wrote with great intimacy and familiarity about our natural world: "Praised be You, my Lord, with all your creatures, especially Sir Brother Sun....Praised be you, my Lord, through Sister Moon and the Stars....Praised be You, my Lord, through Brother Wind, and through the Air, cloudy and serene, and every kind of weather....Praised be You, My Lord, through Sister Water...through Brother Fire...through our Sister Mother Earth....". He identifies God with created things and saw the handprint of the Divine in all of nature.[482] The concern for the ecology, for the welfare of the planet, may be functioning at the present time as an avenue for development of a global spirituality. Earth Day is celebrated all over the World, and Environmentalists everywhere preach much the same doctrines: rescue from pollution, recycling, thinking as a bioregion, respect for the dignity and beauty of the earth, identifying with the planet as a whole, setting aside human in-group greediness to reach out to the needy and to other species. There are common spiritual values, common spiritual insights in all these movements. They are bound to grow stronger and more explicit, because the problems that provoked them are real

---

480 Charles birch, William Eakin and Jay B. maryknoll, *Liberating Life* (New York: ORBAS Books, 1990), 151.

481 Ibid., 153.

482 *Joe Nangle, A Spirituality of Ecology (Washington D C: OFM, 2004),* 205.

everywhere and are also growing.[483] Elisabet Sahtouris has picked up this idea and developed it with the theme that "the Earth is a live planet rather than a planet with life upon it." She calls us to understand ourselves as "living beings within a larger living being, in the same sense that our cells are part of each of us."[484]

The cosmos is God's 'womb', as it were. The intimate relationship between God and the cosmos explodes with seminal energy that generates and regenerates life. God, as it were, energises the cosmos and the cosmos in return dances with the Creator.[485]

## B. 2. Mission Concern

All beings in nature are citizens, have rights, and deserve respect and reverence, human beings must feel that they are sons and daughters of the rainbow. All created beings must look for new relationships of kindness, compassion, cosmic, solidarity, and deep reverence for the mystery that each one bears and reveals. Only then, there will be integral liberation of the human being and of earth, and rather than the cry of the poor and the cry of the earth there will be common celebration of the redeemed and the freed, human beings in our own house, on our good, great and bountiful Mother Earth.[486]_

The lack of this eco-consciousness and its penetration in daily life in the society is a serious phenomenon in realization of our mission. Concern must be shown, (a) on renunciation of greed and (b) fulfilment in the minimum needed for life. Religion demands a simple way of life which gives content with fewer needs.

Pope John Paul II states: "Modern society will find no solution to the ecological problem unless it takes a serious look at its lifestyle.... Simplicity, moderation and discipline ... must become part of everyday life, lest all suffer the negative consequences of the careless habits of a few".

---

483 Alan Atkisson, *The Eco Solution* (Michigan: Zondervan , 1990), 48.

484 Pope John Paul II, *Message for the world Day of Peace*, 1990, 13.

485 Desmond De Sousa, "Towards a Christian Perspective on Environment and Ecology", *Vidyajyoti*, 58 (1994), 589.

486 L. Boff, *Cry of the Earth, Cry of the Poor* (New York: Maryknoll, Orbis, 1997), 114.

Primarily our mission concern should cover the whole cosmos. God is present in every created reality and he takes care of all creatures. R. J. Raja says, "The fact that God not only creates, protects and perfects all the creatures but also indwells, accompanies, participates and delights in them, calls for a relationship of mutuality between creatures and us humans".[487]

If we read Matthew 25 in a new light Jesus says, "Just as you did it to one of the least of these who are members of my family, you did it to me" (25:40). Thus, the other creatures should be considered as our family members and whatever we do to assert their rights, to care for them lovingly, and to look after them tenderly would amount to doing good to God, who is present in them.The indigenous people of India are generally related more closely to the Mother Earth. For example, one can observe that the *Juangs* of Orissa, *Muria Gonds* of Bastar, *Munda* of Jharkhand all have reverence for Mother Earth. In fact, the whole of a life cycle — birth, growth, occupation, marriage, death — all are related to the Earth. Since tribal life revolves around the earth, they treat her as their own preserver, protector, progenitor and above all the most revered and respected Mother. Their consideration of the Earth is: "Our territories and forests are to us more than an economic resource. For us, they are life itself and have an integral and spiritual value for our communities". [488] This concept of treating the Earth as Mother should be in our spiritual depth and in our conscious living, so that our life has respect and veneration towards this Mother, through whom we cherish the love of the Divine.

## B. 3. Ecological Spirituality to Sustain Ecological Stability

When human experience the spiritual transformation, they are given the spiritual power to fulfil the role of modelling and exercising responsible stewardship. When human is able to live under the authority of God, they are given the potential to serve nature and uphold God's rule over Creation, working against the threats of

487 R. J. Raja, "Eco-challenges from the Bible," *Word & Worship Vol. 30* (March - 1997), 321.

488 Johnson Vadakumchery, "*The Earth Mother and the Indigenous People of India*", *Journal of Dharma*, 18/1 (1993), 97.

violence to nature. Human existence on this planet may be considered as a probationary period. It is part of human probation to learn to get context over man's desires and maintain the fruitfulness of the Earth. One must have the willingness to risk changing the way one do things in order to honour God, fellow-man and the Creation.

It involves a new spiritual and even mystical communion with the Earth, a true aesthetic of the Earth. Sensitivity to Earth needs a valid economy of the Earth. We need a spirituality that emerges out of a reality deeper than ourselves, even deeper than life, a spirituality that is as deep as the Earth process itself, a spirituality born out of the solar system and even out of heavens beyond the solar system.[489]

## C. Understanding Spirituality in Handling Ecological Problems

### C. 1. Not Ownership, but Stewardship

Our mastery over nature and our potential for development are to be seen in the context of our relationship with the Creator and also with the entire Creation. We have no ownership over the Creation; God is the owner of all. Our authority over nature in enjoying the fruit of the Earth is more of a trustee than an owner. Our responsibility then is to exercise our stewardship. We need to exercise our stewardship in a responsible way to properly maintain nature's capacity to serve its intended purpose. The fruit of the Earth is to be the source of nourishment and strength to humanity and other Creation. Our stewardship includes all aspects of maintaining the fruitfulness of the Earth. We need to take action to prevent anything that destroys this fruitfulness. While we take from nature, we also need to remember to give back to nature what it needs to supply the needs of the future.[490]

---

489 Thomas Berry, *"the spirituality of the Earth"*, Liberating life; contemporary Approaches to ecological theology. (Ed:) Charles Birch,William Ealvin, Jay B. McDaniel. Orbis Books, New york (1990), 151.

490 Dr. George Samuel, *Eco-Development and Nature Conservation* of *Understanding spirituality in Handling Ecological Problems*, Edited by K. P. Joy (New Delhi: AIACHE, 1994), 126-127.

## C. 2. Spiritual Principles to maintain Ecological Balance

Human, through its rebellion and distorted relationship afflicted wounds on Creation. The setting right of these relationships is not only a sociological function, but also a spiritual operation. We need to adhere to these spiritual principles in order to establish a peaceful co-existence with other Creation as mention below:[491]

*Interdependence*: The Earth is an interdependent community of life. All parts of this system are interconnected and essential to the functioning of the whole.

*The Value of Life*: Life is sacred. Each of the diverse forms of life has its own intrinsic value.

*Beauty*: Earth and all form of life embody beauty. The beauty of the Earth is food for the human spirit. It inspires human consciousness with wonder, joy and creativity.

*Humility:* Human beings are not outside or above the community of life. We have not woven the web of life; we are but a strand within it. We depend on the whole for our very existence.

*Responsibilities*: Human beings have a special capacity to affect the ecological balance. In awareness of the consequences of each action, we have a special responsibility to preserve life in its integrity and diversity and to avoid destruction and waste for trivial or merely utilitarian reasons.

*Rights:* Every human being has the right to a healthy environment. We must grant this right to others: both, those living today and the generation to come.

## Implications

If the ecological devastation is a moral and a social problem, the solution should also concern the moral and social spheres. Therefore, spirituality calls for attitudinal and structural changes in both these spheres, especially in areas actively involved in polluting the Earth.

---

491 Dr. George Samuel, *Eco-Development and Nature Conservation* of *Understanding spirituality in Handling Ecological Problems*, Edited by K. P. Joy (New Delhi: AIACHE, 1994), 126-127.

The first is a renunciation of greed and fulfilment in the minimum needed for life. Religion demands a simple way of life which goes content with fever needs. Pope John Paul II states:

> Modern society will find no solution to the ecological problem unless it takes a serious look at its life style... Simplicity, moderation and discipline, must become part of everyday life, lest all suffer the negative consequences of the careless habits of a few.[492]

A call to change is a call to take sides with what is right and to hate evil. A form of awareness is to be created in all the people so that a hatred of "eco-devastation and a liking for eco restoration may be created. An education in ecological responsibility is urgent". In order to strive for the wholeness of Creation, the following recommendations are made.[493]

- That it should be realized that God cannot be loved served, apart form the whole cosmos (nature and Creation).
- The Church should re-state and re-affirm the presence of the spirit of God in the whole Creation and in Jesus Christ, the new Creation.
- The Church should perceive and also communicate through her life-style, the truth that the Earth is a sacrament, where God's presence is manifest, when God's transcendence and immanence ought to be recognized.
- The Church has to promote an action – oriented spirituality which seeks to resist all forms of oppression and destruction of living things in the Earth and to seek justice.

## Conclusion

The size of our ecological problem is immense. Our task is difficult and big. We need to live in the world with the vision of 'the co-operative commonwealth' or love, love justice, righteousness and

492 John Kulanda, "Basics in Eco-Spirituality" *VJTR* Vol. 56 (1992), 500.

493 Ibid., 501.

peace, which humankind has in its power to bring about. Our search is not just for spirituality *per se* or for spirituality as such, but for a spirituality that is authentic and meaningful.

# Bibliography


Atkisson, Alan. *The Eco Solution.* Michigan: Zondervan,1990.

Ali, Mohammad Imran. "Legal Protection for the Minorities in India." *Legal News & Views* 19/10 (October, 2005), 10-11.

Alston, William P. "Religious language". *The Encyclopedia of Philosophy.* Edited by Paul Edwards, Vol.7. New York: The Macmillan Comp & the Free Press, 1967.

Aleaz, K. P. *The role of Pramanas in Hindu-Christian Epistemology.* Calcutta: Punthi Pustak, 1991.

Atkinson, James. "Atonement." In *A Dictionary of Christian Theology.* Edited by Alan Richardson London: SCM Press, 1969, 18-24.

Aulen, Gustav. *Christus Victor: A Historical Study of the Three Main Types of the idea of Atonement.* London: SPCK, 1931.

Birch, Charles, William Eakin and Jay B. Maryknoll. *Liberating Life.* New York: Orbis Books, 1990.

Boff, L. *Cry of the Earth, Cry of the Poor.* New York: Maryknoll, Orbis Books, 1997.

Baillie, D. M., *God was in Christ: an Essay on Incarnation and Atonement.* London: Faber and Faber Ltd., 1961.

Berkouwer, G. C. *Studies in Dogmatics: the Person of Christ.* Michigan: WM .B. Eerdmans Pub., Company, 1954.

Barth, Karl. *Church Dogmatics*. Vol. 2 Part II. Edinburgh: T &T Clark, 1963.

Berkouwer, G. C. *The Triumph of Grace in the Theology of Karl Barth.* Grand Rapids: WM. B. Eermans Pub., Comp. 1956.

Braaten, Carl. *History and Hermeneutics* . Philadelphia: Fortress Press, 1966, 131, cited by Duncan S. Fergusan, *Biblical Hermeneutics: An Introduction*. Atlanta: John Knox Press, 1986.

Bultmann,Rudolf. "New Testament and Mythology", in *Kerygma and Myth: A Theological Debate*. Ed. Hans-Werner Bartsch. London: SPCK, 1972.

Bose, Nirmal Kuma *Tribal Life In India*. New Delhi: National Book Trust, 1971.

Bhowmik, K. L. *Tribal India: A Profile in Indian Ethnology*. Calcutta: The world Press Private Ltd., 1986.

Brown, Colin. *Philosophy and the Christian Faith.*London: Inter-Varsity Press, 1969.

Copleston, F. C. *Aquinas*. Middlesex: Penguins Books, 1961.

Chaudhury, Dipanjan Roy. "Another Quota Row." *Indian Current* 18/17 (April, 23, 2006): 24-29.

Christian Conference of Asia. *No Place in the Inn: Voices of Minority peoples in Asia*. Tokyo: Christian Conference of Asia, 1979.

Cullman, Oscar. *The Christology of the New Testament*. Philadelphia: The Westminster Press, 1959.

Cone, James H. *God of the Oppressed.* New York: The Seabury Press, 1975.

Cone, James H. *For My People: Black Theology and Black Church.* Maryknoll, New York: Orbis Books,1984.

Cone, James H. *A Black Theology of Liberation*. Maryknoll, New York: Orbis Books, 1986.

Clark, Alden H. *The Social Dynamics of Jesus*. Madras: Christian Literature Society, 1930.

Consultation Findings. "The Mission of the Church and the Development of Tribal Communities in

India Today". *Religion and Society* 9/4 (December, 1962), 81-100.

Dillistone, F. W. "Atonement." In *A New Dictionary of Christian Theology*. Edited by Alan Richardson & John Bowdon. London: SCM Press, 1983, 50-53.

Daly, Mary. *Beyond God the Father: Towards Philosophy of Women's Liberation*. London: Women's Press, 1986.

Dube, S. C. *Tribal Heritage of India: Ethnicity, Identity and Interaction,* Vol. 1. New Delhi: Vikas Pub., House, 1977.

Das, S. T. *Tribal Life of North- Eastern India: Habitat, Economy, Customs and Traditions.* Delhi: Gain Publishing House, 1986.

Fuller, Reginald H. & Pheme Perkins. *Who Is This Christ?* Philadelphia: Fortress Press, 1983.

Gnanadasan, Aruna. *Theology of Humanhood.* Delhi: ISPCK, 1986.

Ghosh, S. K. *Protection of Minorities and Scheduled Castes.* New Delhi: Ashish Pub., House, 1980.

Gupta, Anil. K. "Think about the poor." *The Week* 24/21 (April 23, 2006), 14.

Gilson, Etienne. *The Spirit of mediaeval Philosophy*, translated by A. H. C. Downes. New York: Charles Scribner's Sons, 1940.

Gilson, Etienne. *History of Christian Philosophy in the Middle Ages.* London: Sheed and Ward, 1955.

Grensted, L. W. *The Atonement in History and in Life: A Volume of Essays*. London: SPCK, 1929.

Grenz, Stanley J. & Roger E. Olson. *20th Century Theology: God and world in a Transitional Age*. Illinois: IVP, 1992.

Hrangkhuma, F. "Christ and Tribal Culture", in *Christ and Culture*, eds., Jacob Kavunkal & F. Hrangkhuma. Bombay: St. Paul's Press, 1994.

Hick, John H. *Philosophy of Religion.* New Jersey: Prentice-Hall, INC, 1963.

Hankey, W. J. *God in Himself: Aquinas Doctrine of God as Expounded in the Summa Theologiae.* Oxford: Oxford University Press, 1987.

Hughes, Thomas Hywel. *The Atonement: Modern Theories of the Doctrine*. London: George Allen & Unwin Ltd., 1949.

Hughes, Philip. *The Church in Crisis: A History of the Twenty Great Councils*. London: Burns & Oates, 1961.

Harris, H. "German Liberation". In the *New Dictionary of Theology*. Ed. Allan Richardson. Illinois: IVP, 1994.

Jha, Suman K. & Debashish Mukherji. "Don't quota me!" *The Week* 24/21 (April 23, 2006), 12-14.

Jeanrond, Werner G. *Theological Hermeneutics: Development and Significance*. London: Macmillan Press Ltd., 1991.

Jeremias, Joachim. *Jerusalem in the Time of Jesus: An Investigation into Economic and Social Conditions during the New Testament Period*. London: SCM, 1969.

Kumar, Abhijeet. "Internal reservations for SC/ST." *Dalit Voice* 25/10 (May 16-31, 2006), 9.

Kelly, J. N. D. *Early Christian Doctrines*. New York: Harper & Brothers, 1960.

Kung, Hans. *Great Christian thinker*. London: SCM Press Ltd, 1994.

Knudson, Albert C. *The Doctrine of Redemption*. New York: Abingdon-Cokesbury Press, 1933.

Kelly, J. N. D. *Early Christian Doctrines*. London: Adam & Charles Black, 1958.

Kegley, Charles W. ed. The Theology of Rudolf Bultmann. London: SCM Press, 1966.

Kappen, Sebastian. *Jesus and Freedom*. Maryknoll, New York: Orbis Books, 1977.

Kappen, Sebastian. *Jesus and Culture*. Delhi: ISPCK, 2002.

Kasemann, Ernst. *Jesus Means Freedom: A Polemical Survey of the New Testament*, translated by Frank Clarke. London: SCM Press LTd, 1969.

Keitzar, Renthy. *In Search of Relevant Gospel Message*. Guwahati: Christina Literature Centre, 1995.

Lane, Tony. *The Lion Concise Book of Christian Thought.* Tiruvalla: Suvartha Books, 1984.

Leff, Gordon. *Medieval Thought: From St. Augustine to Ockham.* Middlesex: The Campfield Press, 1958.

Langley, Myrtle. *Equal Women: A Christian Feminist Perspective.* Hants: Marshall Morgan & Scott, 1983.

Longchar, A Wati. *The Traditional Tribal Worldview and Modernity.* Jorhat: N. Limala, 1995.

Longchar, A Wati. *The Traibal Religious Traditions in North East India: An Introduction.* Jorhat: Eastern Theological College, 2000.

Longchar, A Wati "The Need For Doing Tribal Theology", in *Tribal Theology: A Reader*, ed., Shimreingam Shimray. Jorhat: Tribal Study Centre, 2003.

Marrou Henry, *Men of Wisdom: St Augustine and his influence through the Ages.* London: Longmans, n.d.

McIntire, C. T. "Freewill and Predestination Christian Concepts", *in the Encyclopedia of Religion*, edited by Mircea Eliade, Vol.V. New York: Macmillan Pub. Company, 1987, 422-429.

Mackintosh, H. R. *The Doctrine of the Person of Jesus Christ.* Edinburgh: T. & T. Clark, 1912.

Marshall, I. Howard. "To find out what God is saying: reflections on the authorizing of Scripture". In *Disciplining Hermeneutics: Interpretation in Christian Perspective.* Edited by Roger Lundin. Grand Rapids: William B. Eerdmann Pub. Comp., 1997.

Michael, S. M. "What do we Mean by the term Culture?" in *Christ and Culture,* edited by Jacob Kavunkal and F. Hrangkhuma. Bombay: St. Paul's Press, 1994.

Mitra, Bijitendra Mohan *Codification of Tribal Customary Laws.* Kolkata: The Indian Anthropological Society, 2003.

*Nangle, Joe. A Spirituality of Ecology. Washington D. C.: OFM,* 2004.

Nallappan, Francis. "Hindutva and the Minorities: communalism and Discipleship." in *In the Shadow of the Cross.* Edited by Joseph Mattam & Reuben Gabriel. Mumbai: St. Pauls, 2002.

Nida, Eugene A. *Customs, Culture and Christianity*. London: The Tyndale Press, 1954.

Niebuhr, H. Richard. *Christ and Culture*. New York: Harper & Brothers, 1951.

Palley, Claire. "Constitutional Law and Minorities." in *Readings on Minorities: Perspectives and Documents*. Vol. I. Edited by Iqbal A. Ansari. New Delhi: Institute of Objective Studies, 1996.

Pachauri, Pankaj. "The Great Debate: Mandal Commission." *India Today* 15/18 (Sep.16-30, 1990), 39.

Paul, Robert S. *The Atonement and the Sacraments*. New York: Abingdon Press, 1960.

Philip, T. M. *The Encounter between Theology and Ideology: An Exploration into the Communicative Theology of M. M. Thomas*. Madras: Christian Literature Society, 1986.

Rakoczy, Susan. *In Her Name: Women Doing Theology*. Picter Maritzherg: Chester Publication, 2004.

Raj, Udit. "A Sure Pill for Progress." *Indian Current* 18/17 (23, April, 2006), 31-33.

Rajshekar, V. T. "Will not Caste annihilation demand make us enemy of caste-based reservation?" *Dalit Voice* 25/5 (March1-15, 2006), 6-9.

Rashdall, Hastings. *The Idea of Atonement In Christian Theology*. London: MacMillan and Co., 1920.

Richards, G. "Paul Tillich and Inter Religious Dialogue." *Bulletin of Rama Krishna Mission* Vol. 27 (1976), 225-231.

Ramm, Bernard. *Protestant Biblical Interpretation: A Textbook of Hermeneutics*. Grand Rapids: Bakers Book house, 1970.

Ricoeur, Paul. *Essays on Biblical Interpretation*. Ed. Lewis S. Mudge. London: SPCK, 1981.

Robinson, James M. "Hermeneutics since Barth". In *The New Hermeneutics*. Ed. James M. Robinson and John B. Cobb, Jr. Vol. 2. London: Harper and Row Publishers, 1964.

Rayan, Samuel . " Early Christianity as Counter- Culture" in *Religion, Ideology and Counter Culture*, edited by Philip Mathew & Ajit Muricken. Bangalore: Horizon Books, 1987.

Samuel, George. *Eco-Development and Nature Conservation* of *Understanding spirituality in Handling Ecological Problems*. New Delhi: AIACHE, 1994.

Sengupta, Santosh Chandra. *Logic of Religious Language*. Calcutta: Prajna, 1978.

Sobrino S. J., John. *Christology at the Cross reads: A Latin American Approach*. London: SCM, 1978.

Sorabjee, Soli J. "Minorities: National and International Protection." in *Readings on Minorities: Perspectives and Documents*. Vol. I. Edited by Iqbal A. Ansari. New Delhi: Institute of Objective Studies, 1996.

Schaff, Philip. *History of the Christian Church: Nicene and post Nicene Christianity*. Vol. III, Michigan: WM. D. Erdmann's Pub. Comp., 1910.

Schaff, Philip. *History of the Christian Church : Nicene and post Nicene Christianity*. Vol. V. Grand Rapids: WM. B. Eerdmans Pub., Com., 1907.

Samartha, S. J. *One Christ Many Religions: Towards a Revised Christology*. Maryknoll: Orbis Books, 1991.

Samuel, V. C. *The Council of Chalcedon Re-examined: A Historical an Theological Survey*. Madras: The Christian Literature Society, 1977.

Sugden, Chris. *Gospel, Culture and Transformation*. Oxford: Regnum Books International, 1997.

Sumithra, Sunand. *Revolution as Revelation: A Study of M. M. Thomas's Theology.* New Delhi: Theological Research and Communications Institute, 1984.

Tillich, Paul *Dynamics of Faith*. New York: Harper & Row, publishers, Inc., n.d.

Tillich, Paul *Systematic Theology.* I, Chicago: University of Chicago Press, 1951.

Tillich, Paul. *A History of Christian Thought*. London: SCM Press Ltd. 1968.

Tillich, Paul. *Christianity and the Encounter of the world Religions*. New York: Columbia University Press, 1963.

Thomas, M. M. *The Christian Response to the Asian Revolution*. London: SCM Press LTD, 1966.

Thomas, M. M. *The Acknowledged Christ of Indian Renaissance*. Madras: Christian Literature Society, 1970.

Thomas, M. M. *Salvation and Humanization: Some Crucial Issues of the Theology of Mission in Contemporary India*. Madras: Christian Literature Society, 1971.

Thomas, M. M. *The Secular Ideologies of India and the Secular Meaning of Christ*. Madras: Christian Literature Society 1976.

Thomas, M. M. *Revolution in India and Christian Humanism*. New Delhi: Forum for Christian Concern for People's Struggle, 1978.

Thomas, M. M. *Religion and the Revolt of the Oppressed*. Delhi: ISPCK, 1981.

Thomas, M. M. *Risking Christ for Christ's Sake: towards an ecumenical theology of pluralism*. Geneva: WCC Publications, 1987.

Thomas, M. M. *The Church's Mission and Post-Modern Humanism*. Tiruvalla & Delhi: Christava Sahitya Samithi (CCS) & ISPCK, 1996.

Usog, Carmelita. "Women's spirituality for justice" *Ecclesia of women in Asia: Gathering the voices of the Silence*. Delhi: ISPCK, 2005.

Virkler, Henry A. *Hermeneutics: Principles and Process of Biblical Interpretation*. Grand Rapids: Bakers Books, 1981.

Vashum, Yangkahao "Sources For Studying Tribal Theology", in *Tribal Theology: A Reader*, ed., Shimreingam Shimray. Jorhat: Tribal Study Centre, 2003.

Verma, R. C. *Indian Tribes Though the Ages*. New Delhi: publication division, Ministry of Information and Broadcasting, Govt. of India, 1995.

Vidyarthi L. P. & B. K. Rai, *The Tribal Culture of India*. New Delhi: Concept Pub., Comp., 1985.

Wright, D. F. "Augustine", in *the Dictionary of Theology*, edited by Ferguson & D. F. Wright. England: IVP, 1988, 61-63.

Wilson, William E. *The Problem of the Cross: A Study of the New Testament Teaching*. London: James Clark & Co., limited, 1929.

Wingren, Gustaf. *Theology in Conflict: Nygren-Barth-Bultmann*. Translated by Eric H. Wahlstrom. Philadelphia: Muhlenberg Press, 1958.

Wenham, David. *The Parables of Jesus: Pictures of Revolution*. London: Hodder & Stoughton, 1989.

Wolters, Hielke T. *Theology of Prophetic Participation: M. M. Thomas Concept of Salvation and the Collective Struggle for fuller Humanity in India.* Delhi: ISPCK, 1996.

# Index

**R**



**S**



**T**



**U**



**V**



**W**